PIECES *of the* MASTER

Sue Alexander

PIECES *of the* MASTER

For We are All Masterpieces

TATE PUBLISHING *& Enterprises*

Published by Tate Publishing & Enterprises, LLC
127 E. Trade Center Terrace | Mustang, Oklahoma 73064 USA
1.888.361.9473 | www.tatepublishing.com

Tate Publishing is committed to excellence in the publishing industry. The company reflects the philosophy established by the founders, based on Psalm 68:11,
"The Lord gave the word and great was the company of those who published it."

Cover design by Lance Waldrop
Interior design by Nathan Harmony

Published in the United States of America

ISBN: 978-1-60696-313-5
1. Religion: Christian Life: Spiritual Growth
09.04.08

Acknowledgments

I wish to thank first and foremost our God for inspiring me, giving me the dedication to write this book, and for leading Tate Publishing to me.

I also thank all the staff at Tate Publishing for being so kind and helpful.

I thank all the people who prayed for this to happen.

I thank my wonderful husband for all his encouragement and typing and patience. I thank him for his love.

I thank our beautiful children and grandchildren for their support.

I thank the Rossi family for the use of their quiet summer home for me to write.

I thank my very supportive family and friends for all their prayers and love.

Table of Contents

Introduction

This book tells of one who struggled in every relationship until she first established a healthy relationship with God and herself.

Since we are far more than just physical entities, we need to unite our physical with our spiritual to the point that they are always one and evenly balanced. In our physical world, it is difficult to achieve and sustain this balance. I am not suggesting that we lose our physical to our spiritual. I am stating, however, that we all need to find a balance between the two to allow life to work for us instead of against us. When we are successful in uniting the two, we enable ourselves to reap the rewards that far exceed the physical—we get heaven on earth; we get God's angels as our bodyguards; we get Jesus as our Savior and teacher; we get glorious peace of mind. We can search for the things we need and want, but only by uniting our physical with God's spirit do we get them—and more.

I know firsthand how people can knock themselves out trying to be everything to everyone and run into nothing but frustration, pain, and trouble. I know the pain of loving too much. I know the emptiness that was always there in spite of all my genuine efforts to fulfill and be fulfilled. I know there are plenty of people like me for I have met many of them. I know many of them are still struggling.

I am writing this because I have been blessed with guidance to a better way—a way that works. It is incredibly sad to realize how many years I lost to ways that did not work.

Although I have earned no letters to place after my name that identify me as a *professional* and I have no impressive tangible *credentials*, I am a person who is probably very much like you. I am a person whose role in this life does count and I do have something to share.

The essence of my message is I have learned because I have been open and honest with God. The more of myself I have taken to God, the better I have become, and the better my life works.

Everyone moves at a different pace. Everyone tunes in with God as they understand him. Everyone has his or her own comfort level with God. My time had come. It was time for me to do some serious soul searching to find my comfort level with myself and with my God. It is my intention to illustrate what things did not work, why they did not work, and reveal the evolution that has taken me, and my life, to a workable and ever-ascending plateau. This book portrays one who came from fear and inadequacy to self-respect and self-appreciation. Emptiness is no longer my insufferable yet constant companion and I am steadily working toward healthy self-love.

> *Inspiration and encouragement shared, one heart touching another with love, gives birth to incredible happenings.*

I feel the need to share my journey from existing to *living*. For me to have come so far and not share the treasures I have received would be an insult to the source of these treasures. From my heart to your heart may this lead you to a healthier and happier you.

> Originality does not consist in saying what no one has ever said before, but in saying what you think yourself.
>
> James Stevens

> There is a time for everything,
> And a season for every activity under heaven.
>
> Ecclesiastes 3:1

> Thought is a tremendous living force … Thought gains strength by repetition … Thought molds your character and shapes your destiny … Therefore center your thoughts on God and sublime truths.
>
> Sivananda

Throughout this book I will be talking about God. I am not talking about religion. I don't follow any certain organized religion, doctrine, or ritual. I am simply a Christian and I know there is a power greater than any human power; I feel it. It is my lifeline.

I believe in God, the Bible, and I believe that God walked this earth in the human form of Jesus Christ to prove his great love for us and to illustrate the way he intended us to live. At no time do I profess to be a theologian. What I am offering is my perceptions of the Lord as I have come to understand him.

Chapter One

Surrender

Because I knew no better, I spent the first thirty-six years of my life enduring—battling only to survive. I struggled. I resented. I hurt. I hid pain under anger. I attracted dysfunctional relationships. I was always empty inside. No matter how hard I tried and no matter how much I cared, loved, and gave of myself, I kept coming up empty. I had no good things to show for all the trying I did. I had no good feelings about myself or anyone else.

My outlook on relationships and life was cold, pessimistic, and growing more bitter. I felt the only safe way for me to survive was to shut out everything and everyone except my children whom I dearly love. I put a safe distance between others and myself. Caring had become too risky, too painful. Of course, this didn't work either. Nothing worked. I was ugly!

I sought therapy. I prayed. I told God what I needed and how I wanted my life to be. It didn't happen. My life was not working. Then in sheer desperation I told God, "Okay, *I give up!*" This surrendering was the smartest thing I had ever done. I developed an insatiable hunger for books. I craved knowledge. I devoured every spiritual/self-help book I could get my hands on. Each book taught me something valuable—something that I needed to learn. To this day, my reading is a daily shot of encouragement and inspiration.

Melody Beattie taught me, although I dislike the term codependent, that I am indeed codependent. After reading her marvelous books *Codependent No More*, *Beyond Codependency*, and *Codependent's Guide to the Twelve Steps*, I not only recognized and admitted my codependent characteristics but saw that I had been growing and making progress in changing these characteristics into new and healthier traits. She helped me to see where I had come from, where I was now, and encouraged me to grow. She writes from her heart and has something to say to all of us.

Louise Hay, author of *You Can Heal Your Life*, showed me how my specific thought patterns influenced my health and circumstances in my life. Her well-placed humor is delightful, and her enthusiasm for life is contagious.

Bernie Siegel, M.D., in his book, *Love, Medicine & Miracles*, encourages us to recognize and accept the power with which our spiritual conviction dictates the function of our physical bodies. It is my opinion that this book should be required reading for all of humanity.

Wayne Dyer, in his book *You'll See It When You Believe It*, introduced me to the idea of detachment. The ability to detach is extremely valuable. It has served me well. It allows me to separate a person from their behavior.

Barry A. Ellsworth, *Living in Love*, helped me to see that I had become addicted to trouble and to things that did not work.

Og Mandino (I have read every one of his wonderful works) held me spellbound with his stories of believing in miracles. His writings, especially *The Choice* and *The Christ Commission*, have helped my faith to grow immensely.

Marjorie Holmes, *Two from Galilee*, *Three from Galilee*, and *The Messiah*, gave real live to Jesus and many other characters in the Bible. She provides the means for me to come to know and love the Lord in a very personal sense.

Norman Vincent Peale, *You Can if You Think You Can*, shares his gift of integrating traditional and innovative ideas providing wise and viable precepts for a splendid life.

Emmet Fox helped me to understand the greatest teacher of all, Jesus Christ. He walked me through the scriptures in his works *The Ten Commandments* and *The Sermon on the Mount*. Scriptures that had frightened me and had caused me to feel unworthy became comforting and inspiring. Emmet Fox showed me that the Bible does contain great love, beauty, truth, compassion, and profound wisdom. Despite my honest efforts, I had not been able to grasp these incredible gifts from the Bible before reading the works of Emmet Fox.

The love, wisdom, compassion, and inspiration contained in these books and many others is what God gave me when I gave up. I learned firsthand what Melody Beattie meant when she said surrendering is empowering. How vital this is.

This book is an effort to show you how I am learning to put it all together. I am not promising the reader instant success upon completion of this book. I am not offering quick fixes. What I am aspiring to achieve is a healthy, rational illustration of reality. I am getting better—far better than I ever hoped to become. If I can, anyone can. My life is now working for me. My life is easier and enriched. I am no longer swimming upstream.

I had to do some serious work to find Sue. Now that I have found her, I know that she is deserving. The time I am giving to her is well worth it. The work to find Sue is really not that tedious. Actually it is a delightful adventure; an adventure I now choose to commit to as long as Sue is breathing.

All anyone needs to live a workable, remarkable life is an earnest desire and an open mind. Let's go!

Minds are like parachutes—they only work when open.
Thomas Dewy 1864–1930

Chapter Two

Roadblocks

Our first step is to identify the desires that constitute a successful, workable life and make them our constant goals. Then we need to acknowledge and get rid of the things that prevent us from accomplishing them.

The following is a list of my goals—yours may differ, but I believe most of us want the following:

- To enjoy good health
- To enjoy harmonious relationships
- To enjoy abundance
- To earn our living doing what we enjoy
- To develop and share our talents
- To enjoy good things

- To love who we are
- To love and be loved
- To laugh and play
- To take pride in our work
- To develop a spiritual foundation that holds us up when it would be easy for us to fall
- To demonstrate our faith
- To live as an example of integrity and love

Keeping these goals in mind, the list of excuses of what we don't have in our lives could be endless. Let us not waste any more time acknowledging and commiserating that we don't have all of these things—let's get them!

Chapter Three

Physical, Mental, Spiritual = The Circle

Our physical, mental, and spiritual attributes form a closely-knit circle. Pull a loose thread on any one of them, and the others become unraveled as well. In all that I have read, emphasis is upon achieving wholeness. We are encouraged to take power away from illness and adversity and place that power where it belongs—in God and goodness. Development of the spirit strengthens the mind and that strengthened mind helps the body to function properly. However, if we are just beginning to develop our spirit and, therefore, have not yet successfully united physical, mental, and spiritual, we probably lack the discipline and the ability to make ourselves whole.

Achieving wholeness is a lifelong commitment, and we must start slowly. In the beginning of our journey, we easily confuse cause and effect. Spiritually developed people give no power to illness or adversity. They have identified cause and distinguished it from effect. Hence, there is order to their lives that is reflected in good health, positive thinking, and spiritual attainment. The beginning of growth is not the time to argue the causes and effects of poor health or adversity. It is time to acquire knowledge—knowledge of how we function. This takes time though, so start at the beginning. Before embarking on a new program of self-improvement (just as is recommended before beginning a new program of physical exercise), *get a physical*! Go to a doctor and rule out any physical cause for being out of sorts or mentally bogged down.

Wholeness cannot be achieved if any one of its elements is dysfunctional. All must work in harmony. The best example of physical dysfunction that greatly affects mental health is endogenous depression and or anxiety disorder. Depression has received much attention recently, and this is good. Stress plays a large role in it. And what is an active part of everyone's life? Stress!

Two chapters in this book are devoted to endogenous depression and anxiety disorder because endogenous depression is a very real disease that is caused by a chemical imbalance within the brain. This chemical imbalance hinders the thought process. I am striving to shed light on these disorders so that their symptoms may be readily recognized and their potential for rendering one dysfunctional can be respected. The media has presented various views on this disorder. Talk shows, in an effort to present all aspects of it, often convey incomplete pictures due to their time allotment. The controversy is evident, but an incomplete description is often the result. I have endogenous depression and anxiety disorder. I hope to give a complete account of the disorder as it has affected me. Layman's terms will be used because I am not writing this from a medical expert's point of view; I will be giving a victim's viewpoint.

I did not know I had these disorders until they nearly brought me to ruin as I will explain further on, but they alone can keep your life from working. People cannot achieve their goals if a biological disorder is impairing their thought process.

I have grown incredibly because I have read some wonderful books that have encouraged me to strive to achieve a healthy, necessary balance between the physical and spiritual aspects of my life. Each added something vital to my life. I could not have conceived the gifts that all those wonderful authors worked to share if my thought processes were still distorted.

It is essential to find out if there is indeed a physiological or biological dysfunction that causes you to feel out of control or out of touch with yourself. I do this at the risk of being repetitious, but please understand that nothing in your life will work if this disorder is impairing you. I am giving it extra attention because it is so hard to recognize it within yourself. If you are the victim, you will be the *last* one to realize it.

I displayed physical symptoms that required me to be tested for a brain tumor and multiple sclerosis. When these symptoms of anxiety first came about, I was sure that I had had a stroke.

The first symptom was a tingling sensation or numbness on the left side of my face. This occurred every few hours for about three days. The sensation lasted about five to ten minutes. The sensation was scary, but no other stroke symptoms such pain or one-sided weakness accompanied it. On the third day after the initial onset of the numb/tingling sensation, I was at work. I felt absolutely fine, when suddenly my speech became slurred and incoherent. I sounded like I was drunk. The sensation in my face became constant. My equilibrium was off, and I became extremely clumsy. The left side of my face appeared to sag a bit.

I went to the doctor that night, and he assured me that I had not had a stroke but did order some tests, then referred me to a neurologist who ordered more tests. All tests were negative. After six months of tests, my physician suggested that I see a psychiatrist. Of course, I took great offense to this, for I thought that he thought these debilitating symptoms were just of my imagination.

A month later, I found myself sitting reluctantly across the desk from a psychiatrist. He reviewed the test results and the conclusions of my physician and neurologist. We talked for about five minutes when he said he thought I was suffering (suffering indeed) from depression and anxiety disorder. I rebuked his conclusion and explained that there was nothing in my life that would cause me to be depressed, for you see I made the common mistake of equating unhappiness with depression. My life was not lacking happiness or love; I was just miserable and out of sorts. He then proceeded to explain to me that depression and anxiety disorder are actually caused by a chemical imbalance within my brain and did not necessarily have anything to do with the present events or circumstances in my life.

I told him I was reluctant to take an antidepressant because I believed they caused weight gain and that would make me really depressed. This is when I first heard of Prozac (currently a highly controversial medication). At that time (August of 1989), there was little or no controversy. Only when he told me that one of the few side effects was weight loss did I agree to try it. He also prescribed another medication, Xanax, to relieve the anxiety that was crippling me.

When I left his office with the prescriptions in my hand, I was extremely doubtful that they would help, but I figured I could lose a few pounds. So I told myself I would try it for one month. The psychiatrist explained that it would take up to one month for enough of the Prozac to accumulate in my system to produce any noticeable relief.

Anyway, I was sure that this was really no answer. I was convinced that I was certifiably crazed but *not* depressed, and that one day soon I would slip into the land of total insanity and never come back to this side. At times, this slipping to the other side seemed quite appealing. If what I was experiencing was reality, I was tempted to leave it forever.

Because I had focused on the physical symptoms, I had not noticed the signs of depression that had been with me for a long time. Let me clarify that when this depression/anxiety presented its wicked symptoms, my life, for the first time, was quite good. The previous years had been a nightmare. My father committed suicide when I was fifteen. How I wish he could have gotten the help that I did—I realize now the terrible feelings he must have had. I had divorced after seventeen years of a severely dysfunctional marriage. I was raising three daughters by myself. I'd had four surgeries within three years (one life threatening). My beloved mother died in her sleep at age fifty-seven. But I had come out of all of this ugliness still standing.

Now, at the time I was falling apart, I was engaged to a wonderful man; my brother and sister and their families who had lived hundreds of miles away had moved back home. I liked my life better than I ever had before, so why would depression present itself now? *A major question!* It made no sense to me.

The psychiatrist explained to me that Prozac was developed specifically for *endogenous* depression, and that its function was to stabilize the imbalance with my brain chemistry. If my problems were not the result of a chemical, the Prozac would not alleviate the depression. I lived in fight or flight mode for at least twenty-five years, and when things finally got to normal, I could not shut off the fight or flight chemicals.

About ten days after dutifully taking these medications, I noticed that I had a hard time finishing a meal. I felt full sooner. After about another week I noticed that I had lost five of the ten pounds I wanted to lose. Then I began to notice that upon waking in the morning I got out of bed with more energy. A few days later, I saw the whole world differently.

This was the most incredible part. I had not been able to see what I was experiencing as depression until the depression itself lifted. Within three weeks, I was a new person. This is difficult to explain. I could only acknowledge the symptoms of depression in retrospect—in other words, after they were gone.

I no longer had self-destructive and suicidal thoughts. Although I really wanted to live and had more to live for than ever before, that urge to permanently escape kept nagging me.

My speech became coherent again because my thought patterns had cleared. (I had not realized how muddled my thoughts had been because all that I could experience and express was confusion.) The inability to speak clearly had been so debilitating and embarrassing that I was unable to see that the root of the problem was unclear thinking. As my thought processes cleared, I was able to speak intelligibly, and I was no longer losing my thoughts midstream.

As things became increasingly clearer, I recognized that self-pity is *symptom* of depression and not the cause of it. The dam of rage and anger that was always on the verge of bursting was gone. I stopped looking for a fight. I no longer experienced periods of stupor where I would just sit and exist. I became more patient, and other people's words didn't confuse and aggravate me. My last nerve that had been hanging out and upon which everyone and everything danced was soothed. The need to be left alone, mixed with the fear of being ignored, was gone. The need to run, combined with the inability to move, no longer plagued me.

The most startling of all the relief was that the world became three dimensional again; it no longer lacked depth. I did not realize that everything lacked depth until came it back. I was back in tune and I felt wonderful.

Let me reiterate that I had been experiencing all these depressed feelings, but the biggest and cruelest trait of depression is that it does not let you see these things. You cannot see them until they are gone.

I will not attempt to play doctor or scientist here and explain the origin of endogenous depression, and I do not understand the correlation between depression and anxiety. I am not qualified to give medical facts or opinions. However, as a person who is being successfully treated for these disorders, I am qualified to describe them as they have affected me. I am qualified to state how these medications changed my life.

I am not saying that Prozac, Xanax, or any other medication is a cure-all. There is no such thing. I still feel pain, sadness, indignation, and all of the emotions one should feel. The problems that go with life still occur. But no longer do I waste my energies trying to escape the problems of life. Turbulence can no longer throw me off course. I am now capable of facing and solving problems constructively because Prozac clears my thought processes. As a result, I am able to stay in control of my thoughts and emotions.

After being on Prozac for about six weeks, I started giving my thoughts and my beliefs much consideration. It was clear to me that I had been carrying around too much unhealthy junk. With my newfound ability to think clearly I decided it was time to examine my beliefs and strive to become as healthy as possible.

This is the reason for this book. I have been freed and I have grown tremendously. I realized that whether or not I suffered from depression, my life could stand some serious improvement. My life had just never worked. It was time to find Sue.

I have written about my experience with endogenous depression and anxiety disorder because it is an illness that is not commonly understood. It does not receive appropriate attention, and its potential for rendering one dysfunctional is not sufficiently respected. I have written what I experienced, as I understand it. It is necessary to seek and obtain a proper diagnosis and it is possible to be successfully treated.

Depression is not just in your head. You cannot just make it go away. It is *not* a personal weakness. You *cannot* snap out of it. Sometimes depression is more subtle, and other times it is more obvious. I will list the symptoms of these disorders at the end of this chapter with the hope that if you recognize any of these within yourself you will seek medical attention.

If you are depressed, you cannot make yourself right. I don't care how strong you think you are or how reluctant you are to taking medication. If you are experiencing any depression because of a chemical imbalance, then you absolutely need professional diagnosis and treatment. Your life will improve because the medication clears your head. Then it is up to you to decide how much you will improve yourself and your life from that point.

If you experience none of the characteristics of depression or anxiety disorder, I would still like to share with you the extent to which I have improved the quality of my life. I did this by taking the time and doing the work to find Sue. Although it may not be necessary for you, it was, and will be, essential for me to be properly diagnosed and treated for endogenous depression before I can fix any other part of Sue.

The following is a list of symptoms that I experienced with depression and anxiety disorder. These were my symptoms; those of others may vary.

1. Confusion
2. Slurred speech and transposing of words
3. Incredible anger
4. Periods of blind rage
5. Lack of patience

6. Self-pity
7. Constant fear without cause
8. Inability to sleep
9. Constant need for nap with the inability to sleep soundly or restfully
10. Inability to relax
11. Lack of coordination
12. Thick tongue
13. Forgetfulness
14. Absence of motivation
15. Lack of energy
16. Need to run with inability to move
17. Total lack of self-confidence
18. Thoughts of self-destruction
19. Lack of interest in anything or anyone
20. Change in appetite
21. Fear of trying anything because you know you will screw it up
22. Feeling unloved and unlovable
23. Tremendous fear of rejection
24. Happy one minute and crazed the next
25. General feelings of hopelessness and uselessness
26. Extreme sensitivity to criticism

As I said, I am not a physician and I cannot tell you how many of these symptoms warrant treatment or constitute illness, but these are what I experienced in the depressed or anxious state. These are symptoms that I could only see *after* they were gone.

It is my hope that anyone who has these symptoms or these disorders will be fortunate enough to seek and find qualified medical help and treatment. A qualified psychiatrist will monitor your medication closely. Please don't be afraid of the word psychiatrist. There are very competent and caring individuals whose purpose and talent it is to help.

I cannot convey in mere words the *hell* that depression and anxiety are, nor can I express how glorious it is to have a new life granted to me through successful treatment.

Chapter Four

Relapse

I did not initially plan to include this chapter until I relapsed into depression again because I, *myself,* discontinued Prozac. For putting firsthand information/experience into this book, I suppose the miserable relapse has served its purpose. I remembered that depression was awful, but until I experienced it again, I could not truly appreciate or respect how disabling it is. This not-so-gentle reminder made me more aware of depression and anxiety's debilitating stronghold. Untreated it is a dead end. It is a roadblock to any potential human growth or spiritual development. It will keep you a prisoner in its merciless clutches if you fail to recognize it. It will use ugly disguises to try to trick you into wanting to stay depressed, for to even imagine not being depressed requires more energy than depression will allow you to have.

At the time of this writing, I had been taking Prozac for two years. It cleared the way for me to think rationally. Therefore, I began a serious search for Sue. The progress I made was astounding. I felt good about myself for the first time in my life. My new husband was so proud of my growth. I had been able to release many of the hang-ups and false beliefs that were hindering our relationship and that had been the downfall of so much of my life.

People who had known me for years commented and commended me for my healthier state of being. Each day I felt stronger and more in tune with my surroundings. I had stopped attaching myself to other people's trouble and pain. I began to create. I started writing, which I had wanted to do for as long as I can remember. I designed and sewed dresses—a major accomplishment for me, for due to my persistent lack of patience, I always hated to sew. Now I enjoyed it. My creativity, my inspiration, my patience, and my energy were amazing.

Medication alone did not do this. It only enabled me to control my thoughts. It allowed me to think rationally. I proceeded to work on Sue, which I will discuss later in this book.

In the summer of 1991 (two years of taking Prozac), my husband and I along with my sixteen-year-old daughter took a five-day trip to Colorado to visit my husband's brother and his family. I felt so extremely wonderful that I decided that I must be cured and arbitrarily, without consulting my doctor, stopped taking Prozac. I felt great. It was the first time I had gone anywhere that I was able to just enjoy every moment.

I had no painful past, and I proclaimed that God would take good care of our future. There in the mountains amidst "God's country," I was whole and complete.

I was off the Prozac and felt great!

Then *crash*! I mean big-time *crash*! I first noticed a slight tingling sensation in my face but just blew it off. By the time I had been off the medication for about eight days, I was a mess. It happened so abruptly. I got up in the morning and accomplished some quality writing. I decided to do a little shopping. As I was getting ready, I could feel myself start to speed up. When I got to the store, I knew I was in big trouble. My coordination was gone; I was like a walking disaster—knocking thing off of the shelves. Confusion set in and I had to get home. By the time I checked out of the store and drove home (about two miles) all those wicked symptoms were back. I couldn't speak; I couldn't breathe properly. I was terrified and extremely angry. I was looking for a fight. My family looked at me and backed away. They knew I was out of control. By the time evening rolled around, I was in a stupor. I could only mutter vague responses to questions. Thoughts of self-harm were strong.

I saw my psychiatrist the next day. One look at me, and he knew I was out of it. I rambled and carried on. It was again necessary for him to explain to me why I needed this specific antidepressant medication. In fact, he had to explain it several times, for I could not follow his words. He likened my need for Prozac *for the rest of my life* to a diabetic's need for insulin. As I am writing this, I have now been back on Prozac for about five days. But it is like starting all over again. It will be a while before enough of it accumulates in my system to make a difference. Waiting for this proper accumulation is *hell.* Thankfully, I know that each day will be clearer. As of this moment, I have already given up nearly another week of my life to the debilitation of endogenous depression.

I am not happy that I will require this medication for the rest of my life. I still feel like I should be strong enough to conquer it on my own, but this is not possible for me at this point and probably never will be. My body disables me. Perhaps one day I will see that the biological imbalance is the effect and my deep subconscious is the cause. But right now this doesn't matter for I still have more growing to do. In the mean time, I am very thankful that this medication stabilizes me so that I can grow.

Endogenous depression is not a personal weakness. It is a disorder of biological origin. Endogenous depression is not mental illness; it is a dysfunction whose *symptoms* are mental illness. Efforts to conquer this depression by sheer will, while in a depressed or anxious state, will only augment the symptoms. The frustration and confusion will become increasingly debilitating.

However, although I dislike requiring any medication, I am thankful that it is available to me. It does work. Even when I take Prozac faithfully, I will occasionally be aware that depression and anxiety are still trying to take control. I feel low or I have less energy. If I were not taking medication, the depression would overtake me.

I know that Prozac has received considerable bad press, but I know it works for me. I also know firsthand that it works for two of my three daughters. They suffer without it.

• • • • • • • • • • • • •

So many think depression is a weakness. So many have a hang-up about seeking any remedy that has to do with healing or helping the mind. The mention of mental illness, even if there is a biological or physical reason for it, is still a source of shame to many. These beliefs are from the dark ages. And my family and I are very thankful for the proper diagnosis I received from my very qualified doctors and for the amazing benefits of properly prescribed medication.

Had I not received this treatment, I would either be locked up by now or dead like my father. If any of what I have described sounds anything like your or someone you care about, I implore you to seek professional help. Please don't be afraid. Remember, we need to start our growth by taking the steps to rule out physical causes that can hinder our mental states. Medication (prescribed and over-the-counter), certain foods, beverages, allergies, environmental factors, and occult infection can all contribute to tiredness, irritability, and a general feeling of being out of sorts. Go to the doctor. Healthy minds make healthy bodies, and healthy bodies make healthy minds. Spirit rules both. Mind, body, spirit—the three cannot be separated.

Chapter Five

Anger

Anger is a natural step in the grieving process. Anger is a necessary part of processing pain. Anger is an appropriate response to injustice. Anger needs to be expressed constructively. However, anger was never meant to be a chronic condition itself. Anger should never be stored, for it only smolders and festers; it makes us physically and emotionally sick. Anger is a step, but too often, this is where we get stuck. We get to the angry stage and don't know how to get past it. The feelings of anger may subside temporarily, but until we really work through it to get past it, it becomes a continual defense mechanism. I have a favorite expression that causes my children to roll their eyes when they hear it. The only way *to* it is *though it.* Like all of us, they want to get to the top without going through the middle.

Therefore, let me explain that what I want to consider here is the destructiveness of chronic anger. I am referring to anger that becomes a state of being or a way of life instead of a tool for processing pain. I am talking about perpetual anger that is used for protection from anything or anyone that feels uncomfortable. I want to give attention to the chronically angry person who uses anger to avoid core issues.

1. Rage and fury are explosive and intimidating
2. Wrath seeks a vengeance
3. Resentment is indicative of repression

Chronic anger is a secondary emotion. One nearly always feels something before feeling anger. Anger does not just happen; it is either consciously or unconsciously chosen. It becomes a habit to choose anger as a way of avoiding true emotions such as pain or fear. The habit can become so well ingrained that the underlying causes of anger are constantly avoided.

It is difficult to live with anger whether it comes from you or someone you care about. If anger is an active part of your life, it is unhealthy. Anger blames, anger hurts, anger manipulates, anger justifies, anger intimidates, and anger destroys.

Yet, it is easier to justify anger than it is to admit or face the underlying issue. Anger can be passed off as hereditary. "I have a bad temper; it runs in the family." Bad tempers and chronic anger do not run in families, but families do teach and pass on to generations the habit of using anger to offset emotional pain or fear. Anger is inappropriate when it is used as an escape or defense mechanism. It is a learned response, and because so many of us are taught to be tough and not show emotion, anger is our more accepted recourse.

Find a Feeling—Lose an Attitude

Pure anger accomplishes nothing that is constructive. Anger is detrimental to growth. Anger distorts, it builds, it explodes, then it subsides. Hurt feelings may be temporarily soothed, but the core issues remain unresolved. Because the core issues are not resolved, anger will be used repeatedly. Anger will be necessary every time those unresolved issues arise. Anger is not the issue. Anger is a symptom. Anger will not go away until the issue that it is defending is cured or alleviated. It is not knowing *how* to get past the anger that causes the trouble.

Anger does not work for us; it works against us. It does serve its purpose though, and its purpose is to repress pain or fear, to seek vengeance, and to fool us. What is stronger than pain or fear? Anger. Anger is a warning. It is a danger signal. Anger signals that there is pain or fear somewhere within that needs to be found and processed properly.

For years, I used anger to shield my pain, but it never allowed me to heal my pain. It only intensified my pain. I thought that I was using anger to protect myself, but in all actuality, it used me. When I felt the threat of rejection, I felt fear but skipped right over it and reacted with such blind rage that I caused more rejection. Who wants to be around a crazed, enraged, threatened person? Since I could not rationally process the fear, the rage controlled me. Its power scared me. Yet I just converted that fear into more anger.

Anger seeks a victim. Anger is powerful. We use it to deny painful things within ourselves. Anger's purpose is to protect self, but it needs a victim. Sometimes our anger is directed toward ourselves and is manifested in the forms of ill health, addictions, self-mutilation, and starvation, to name just a few. Anger is often directed at another person. Sadly, that other person is usually someone we love very much. Anger in search of a victim allows us the escape from our responsibility to look within ourselves. We opt for this escape because to look within ourselves is just too painful or scary.

Anger constantly set me up as a victim—a victim of myself, my fears, and my own anger. My misuse of anger made victims of those around me. I could not use anger constructively; I could only abuse its power.

> *The purpose of anger is to help us to recognize and process pain. Anger's purpose is not a means for us to avoid or escape pain, nor is it an excuse to cause pain.*

Anger defeats us. It sets us up to the realization of our fears. If we fear rejection, our rage/anger is so ugly that we drive people away from us. Therefore, our fears materialize, and we need even more anger to protect ourselves.

When anger swells, it is a signal that we should *stop*! *Just stop!*

Stop, look, and listen. Stop the anger. Say "No" to it. You can do it. Just say, "No!" Look at what is underneath it and recognize just what you are feeling. Are you feeling hurt, fear, embarrassment, jealousy, humiliation? Are you feeling threatened or intimidated? Why do you feel the need to protect yourself with anger? What really triggered the anger? Find it. *It wants to be found.*

Why do you think it keeps showing up? Anger is a signal that something needs to be fixed. Listen. Listen to what is going on in your head. Are you seeking a victim? Do you want to punish someone? Do you want to hurt someone?

Stop the anger. Tell God what you are feeling and be honest. He knows anyway. God can take it. Tell him how angry you are and why. Tell him that you know these feelings are destructive. When you are done pouring your anger out to the Lord, ask him to let you feel what he would have you feel. Then sit back for a bit. Then be quieter still and listen to what God is telling you. Learn to listen to your inner voice, which is the voice of our Lord. It will come to you as a thought and/or a feeling.

Learning to listen takes some concentrated effort at first, but the more we call upon it, the more we learn to recognize its soothing voice. The more we feel its comforting presence, the more we will desire it. We will earnestly seek that soothing, comforting, loving voice and that peaceful feeling. Then the power of anger is greatly diminished, and ultimately, it will be obliterated.

> Peace I leave with you; my peace I give to you.
>
> Jesus—John 14:27

We need to take care that we do not give power to our anger. We must take power *away* from anger and give it to the *only* thing more powerful than anger, the love and guidance of God.

Since anger is so superb at covering so many underlying emotions, perhaps now would be a good time to explore some of these emotions. Looking at these possible underlying emotions may cause you to feel angry. Please don't ignore the anger; it really wants to tell you something.

Name the Emotion

Unfortunately, we are not taught or encouraged to learn to identify emotions. Our education system mandates that we are to be taught what types of rocks are in caves, yet it is likely that most of will never explore caves. It is mandatory that we learn about the components of the solar system although most of us will never get closer to it than an airplane can take us. It is also mandatory that we learn about the wars of the world and who won them. Some of us know more about some long-dead war hero that we know about ourselves.

No one is required to teach us how to win the wars within ourselves. It is not mandatory that we explore the infinite components of our minds and imaginations. We are not taught to build our own foundations—sturdy as rocks to support us through the tough stuff. It is nearly impossible to contribute to society, to make use of the knowledge we are presented with in school, if we never develop our own selves first. If we can't identify our own emotions, we cannot process them. We cannot bring them into perspective. When we can't process them, we get *stuck*! Then our potential is greatly hindered. We and our lives do not work right. We need to take the time to learn to recognize what we feel.

Fear Emotions

Read the list of fear emotions below. You may want to add more of your own. Upon reading the list, first become aware of your automatic reaction or write down the first thing you feel when you read the following potential fears.

- We are being rejected.
- We are being laughed at.
- We are not good enough.
- We are being treated in a hurtful manor.
- Our feelings don't matter to others.
- Our needs won't be met.
- Others don't need us for who we really are.
- We may fail.
- We may not know enough.
- We don't look good enough.
- We just aren't enough.
- We may have to change.
- We may have to do something unfamiliar.

Go over the list a second time, this time acknowledging or writing down the worst possible thing that could happen *if* the fear became reality. Then convert that fear to a positive statement.

My biggest fear has been fear of rejection. When I would feel the threat of rejection, my automatic response was rage. The worst did happen; I was rejected—more than once. The rage never fixed it, and I'm still here, in many ways probably better off for it. I took this fear of rejection and all the pain encompassing it and picked it apart. I realized that I was not rejected because I was awful. As time went on, I recognized that those who had rejected me were incapable of making the commitment required to be part of a healthy relationship, and that I did not possess enough knowledge of healthy relationships to make a positive contribution. My positive statement now is, "I am a loving and caring person. I deserve to be loved. I now only attract people that I can love and people who are capable of loving me." It works!

Pain Emotions

Read the following list of pain emotions. Add your own where necessary. Then work them through the same steps.

We may hurt because:

- Someone did not meet our expectations.
- We failed to meet our own expectations.
- Someone physically hurt us.
- Someone did not take our feelings seriously.
- We hurt someone else.
- We did not do the right thing.
- Someone did not love us enough.
- We were too afraid to make our needs known.
- We feel rejected.
- We feel dumb.
- We feel ugly.
- We feel afraid to fail.
- We feel afraid to succeed.
- We feel afraid to try.
- We are afraid to tell someone how we feel.
- We lose someone we love.

Did you see your automatic responses or reactions? Were you able to get past the response or reaction stage and see the healthy action you are capable of taking? Can you see that you don't have to be stuck?

Blaming Others

Now read the blame list and acknowledge or write down who you automatically blame—or who first comes to your mind.

We may blame others when:

- We are bored and no one is entertaining us.
- We feel sad and no one notices.
- We feel sad and no one tries to help.
- We feel overworked and no one helps.
- We feel overworked and no one tries to help.
- We feel overworked and we don't ask for help.
- We are afraid.
- We can't look inside ourselves.
- Others don't read our minds and meet our expectations.
- We fail to meet our responsibilities.
- We see things in others that remind us of ourselves.
- We try to help others and they won't let us.
- We cannot accept one or more of our own characteristics.

Who was it that you blamed the most? Who was the first person who popped into your head as you read each statement above? Why that person? Was or is that person capable of making things better? Whose fears are they? Whose reactions are they? Who is responsible?

The following truth will *never* change:

> *You, and only you, will always be responsible to and for you, and only I can and must be responsible for myself.*

Stop looking out. Start looking in. The answers are there; they always have been. The answers will always be within us. I know this anger system and I know it well. I know how it operates, and after thirty-six years of anger in one form or another, I know *it does not work!*

Chapter Six

Living with Anger

My father was always angry. Only twice in the fifteen years that I knew him did he speak to me in a tone without anger. I was so shocked by the normal tone of his voice that I didn't know what to do. He was always angry. It was not always an explosive anger; sometimes it was a repression that we could only see as great sadness.

At thirty-nine years old, he killed himself. He and my mother were divorcing, and one week to the day before their divorce was to be final, he committed suicide. None of us knew *exactly* what was hidden behind all the anger, nor did any of us know how to get past it. I, personally, was too afraid to try.

He was stuck in anger and stuck in the reaction mode.

He reacted negatively to everything. His anger and his reactions kept him his own prisoner. We all felt like victims. I'm sure he did too. He was only capable of reacting; therefore, he was incapable of taking any action toward health, peace, harmony, and love. The things he so desperately needed, he denied himself because he could not get past anger, and his reactions exhausted him to the point that he had no strength left for healthy action. We were all scared of him. We didn't know how to love him.

Now, in retrospect, I can clearly see that he was doing all that he knew how to do. He possessed great mechanical abilities. He could build anything. He was a very hard worker. He worked hard for us and provided us with the material things we needed. He was only able to show his love for us through his hard work. His anger incapacitated his ability to give or receive love.

He was an only child whose mother died suddenly when he was only seven years old. His father was extremely rigid and cold. The man never smiled. He was incapable of nurturing his son. It was right for my father to be angry when his mother died. But no one took the time or had the ability to take him all the way through the grieving process. He got stuck in fear and anger.

I know he loved us, but he could only show it through his hard work. He could not give love in any other way. He never learned any other way. When his efforts to prove his love for us through hard work left him empty inside, he became angrier because his efforts did not produce what he expected and needed. There is no substitute for love. If we don't learn, encourage, and accept love in our lives, we cannot give it and it is unlikely that we will ever *allow* ourselves to receive it.

He built a fortress around himself and that fortress was anger. He was sending us plenty of messages. Again, they are much clearer in retrospect. None of us knew how to decode these messages and his anger did not encourage us to want to try. Anger expressed through inappropriate and unacceptable behavior ruled our lives. I am not proud or pleased to admit that the only thing I felt when I heard he was dead was relief. The madness of his ever-increasing desperate displays of anger was over. So we buried him and never mentioned his name for sixteen years.

From Madness to Madness

Yes, the noisy, obvious, intrusive madness ended with my father's death, but a more subtle type of madness only took its place. The empty space that appeared when my father died was very quickly and slyly filled with another madness—a different madness, but still madness.

Afraid to ask for fear of the answer

My dysfunctional marriage and its similarities to my parents' dysfunctional relationship had brought me to the point of being crazed. Sixteen years after my father's death and thirteen years into my own first marriage, I was strongly encouraged by a friend to get counseling. After one of my therapy sessions, I revealed to my mother that my sister and I felt relieved when our father died. My mother was shocked! She *assumed* we hated her and blamed her for our father's death.

For sixteen years she *assumed this*! But not once in those sixteen years did she ever ask us how we felt. It didn't occur to us to tell her because we *assumed* she knew. Since she felt that she rejected him, she assumed responsibility for his death, so she sentenced herself to a life of idiopathic hypertension and various other serious illnesses including a stroke, two types of cancer, uremic poisoning, and heart disease. She died in her sleep at age fifty-seven. She was five feet two inches tall. She never smoked, rarely drank, did not drink coffee, and never weighed more than 105 pounds. Eighteen years of testing revealed no physical cause for her chronic hypertension. I watched her destroy herself physically. I could not convince her that she deserved better. She had sentenced herself. We sure weren't ready to lose her.

She never asked us how we felt about our father's death because she was afraid of the answer. She told me this herself. Fear of the *assumed* answer prevented her from asking the question. She reacted to her beliefs but she was never able to take any action to substantiate or alleviate her assumed beliefs. Stuck in reaction mode. What a penalty she sentenced herself to, a life of illness and self-destruction. What a waste.

Now let's go back to the quiet madness that moved in when my father died. My mother remarried two years later. She married a good man who loved her very much. Although she had all reasons to be happy, she could rarely accept happiness for herself. At times, she would radiate love, joy, and life; yet it never lasted. Every episode of happiness was matched with an episode of serious illness. She just could not allow herself to enjoy anything and stay healthy, for it was part of her erroneous self-punishment. Perhaps, just perhaps, if she had received the guidance to resolve her misplaced guilt, she would not have suffered so.

Repeating that which we fail to learn

Three years after my father's death, guess what kind of man I married? You got it; a man who was just like my father! They even lost their mothers at the same age. They were both mechanics and extremely gifted. Both worked in the same places at different times. In the naiveté of my youth, I married this man and created the same life that I was so relieved to lose when my father died. I couldn't rescue my father from his pain, but I was sure I could rescue my husband.

I believed if I just loved him enough and made up for the lack of nurturing in his childhood, I could fix him. His lack of nurturing presented itself as self-pity and the repression of his pain showed itself as anger. Anger dominated our lives. Our life together was totally dysfunctional. We nearly destroyed each other. Understandably, our children learned some pretty unhealthy habits from us in spite of my constant efforts to shield them.

Twelve years into my marriage, I knew I had to get out to even have a chance to be healthy. Fear held me prisoner for another five years. Fear of hurting my husband, fear that he could not survive without me, fear of not knowing what healthy was. Those five years were hell for all of us. It is only by the grace of God that we all made it.

God's grace took us beyond survival. We have healed the sick relationship and started the healing process; I had to make a decision to change. I had to come to honest terms with my fears and my guilt. I had to refuse to take part in any and all unhealthy behavior. I had to decide that anger would no longer control my life. When I did honestly face my fears, one at a time, they didn't seem so overwhelming.

Then, through God's grace, we were able to replace our feelings of bitterness and animosity with the healing power of forgiveness. This did not happen overnight. Thankfully though, about a year after our divorce was final, we agreed to let go of the past and to accept and respect one another's new and separate lives. We both agreed that enough destruction had been done throughout the marriage and divorce. We—and our children—had nothing to gain by holding on to bitterness.

My ex-husband has remarried and his wife is a very lovely lady. I truly like her. I have remarried, and my husband and I are committed to creating a life that works and we are succeeding. I am proud to say that the four of us are able to share special occasions with our children, cooperate in issues involving them, and still show respect for the other's privacy. The four of us often chuckle at the reactions of others when we are together. In view of the bitterness that ruled us for so long, this is nothing short of a miracle.

Desire to Decision

It took a conscious desire, therefore a conscious decision, on my part to seek and achieve a healthy life. That desire could only have come from my higher power, for I certainly had no examples of healthy lives or relationships as a child.

As a young child, I adopted the habit of daily prayer, but I prayed more as if I was placing an order in a restaurant. Yet

I must believe that turning to God for a few minutes every day, even if it wasn't exactly in the proper way, instilled in me the desire to kick the unhealthiness out of my life and to seek life as God would have me live it.

There is still a bit of anger in me, but every day it grows less and less. The remnants of anger are directed at anger itself. I am angry because anger, itself, had the power to take so much from my life, and it could give nothing back. I am angry that I didn't know I could disable anger any time I chose. I am angry that I didn't know better sooner, but to give that anger any power now would be to regress. Therefore, I achieve my inner peace regarding this by remembering that *there is a season and a time for every purpose under heaven.* This allows me to go forward and resist any temptation to go back.

I have learned to automatically recognize anger as a *danger* signal. It is a signal for me to stop, look, and listen. I stop the anger, and the more I successfully stop it, the more power I have over it. It rarely has power over me now.

I look to see what is the underlying emotion. I look at it to see who and what it serves. I tell my feelings to God and I omit nothing regardless of how ugly it is.

Then I listen. I listen for my Lord to guide me. I ask God to let me feel what he would have me feel. I pack up my fears one by one and throw them to the heavens. Then I am free to receive what the Lord is so willing to give me. I receive peace of mind as well as the insight, guidance, and strength to put things back on the right track. I receive an overpowering sense of love and the pain just turns to peace.

Remember This Truth

The Lord is always happy to fill us with good things if only we are willing to let go of the bad.

> Know the truth and the truth shall set you free.
>
> John 8:32

Remember one of the first lessons you learned as a child. Stop, look, and listen before you cross the street. This is a valuable lesson, for it applies to far more than crossing streets.

Learn to recognize anger as a danger signal. Then take the necessary steps to process it. Immense joy will come to you. Things around you start to change for the better and wonders really do happen. It is *glorious!*

Action or Reaction

This is important—differentiating between reaction and action. It is also important to use each in its proper time and place. Each serves a necessary function. Too often one is used for the other. This is trouble.

Chapter Seven

Action vs. Reaction

When you react, you are responding to something. The first thing that pops into your head in any situation is probably your learned response. Are they true responses or are they responses that you learned from others? Are they helping your life to work? Or do they just keep taking you back to the same place? If you aren't sure, just ask yourself, "Is my life working?"

Let's take it a step further. How often do you or does someone close to you overreact? What does reacting and overreacting do for you or this other person? How do you feel when you are reacting or overreacting, or when you are at the mercy of someone who is reacting or overreacting?

Helpless? How comfortable are you with yourself? How comfortable are all the people present?

It is necessary to respond, and it is necessary to react. If you did not respond or react, you would not be human. However, reacting without taking action is as useless and destructive as is acting without thinking. It is just a longer process. If you react without ever taking action, you will either move sideways or spin in circles. You will not break out of the circle though. You must take some intelligent action based upon circumstances and your examined reaction.

Example:

A young man with a wife and child needs a more dependable car. There is an error on his credit report that can be fixed. The error is not his fault. Every time he sees a car that he likes and cannot afford, he does the following:

1. He is attracted to the new car.
2. He becomes more aware of how much he dislikes his present car.
3. His dislike for his present undependable car builds to anger.
4. His want for the new car intensifies his anger.
5. He reacts by yelling, blaming, stomping, etc.
6. His tantrums hurt those around him—namely, his wife.
7. He excuses his anger and frustration by saying, "Well, you know my credit report is messed up."
8. He attempts to soothe the discord and hurt of his tantrums
9. He chills out for a while—kind of goes into neutral.
10. He does not fix his credit report.

Guess what happens a few days later when he sees another car he'd like to buy? You got it. He faithfully repeats steps one through ten.

Stuck

He is stuck in reaction mode. His fear of taking action keeps him stuck. He knows the solution, but he is more comfortable being miserable than he is with taking the necessary action. Because aggravation and misery are more familiar than taking positive action, he chooses misery over action. Those around him are tired of his reaction-without-action-syndrome. He is slowly driving them away, but he needs to feel safe, and he feels safer in his familiar misery than he does in the unfamiliarity of action.

Some actions are simpler and some are more complex. The action required may be as simple as putting a nail into a loose step so you don't have to cuss and fuss every time you trip over it. Or it may be as complex as going to the Supreme Court to achieve an action.

Whatever the complexities of the required action, there is a time to act, and failure to do so is to choose to stay on a roller coaster that never stops.

It is so easy to sit around, stomp around, crab and complain, and then do nothing. There came a time in my life, after being seriously stuck in reaction mode for years, when I had to adopt the following motto for myself. *If you aren't willing to fix it, don't complain about it!*

Often it takes less energy to take the action than it does to display the reaction.

As I said earlier, both reaction and action are necessary, but they must compliment one another. One must never be substituted for the other. If you just keep reacting and never act, you will drive yourself and those who choose to stay around you crazy.

If you are only reacting when you should be acting, anger will show up somewhere. Anger is that d-anger signal that indicates that something needs to be fixed. It is time to stop, look, and listen again.

In our education system, it is mandatory that we, as students, learn many things that we will never really use. However, no one is required to teach us how to take appropriate, intelligent, healthy steps toward personal-problem solving. We are not taught the most valuable lessons; the lessons of how to build a life that works. How are we ever going to get anywhere if, as adults, we have to spend so much of our time learning the basics that we should have been taught in our youth?

Chapter Eight

Addictions

> A fool may be known by six things: Anger without cause; speech without profit; change without progress; inquiry without object; putting trust in a stranger; and mistaking foes for friends.
>
> Arabian Proverb

In truth, we are all addicts of some sort. If this makes you raise your eyebrows in contempt, relax. There is no offense intended here. Our ways of life become habits. Some habits are good and some are bad, and some lifelong habits turn into addictions. In other words, they are very deeply ingrained, and they are familiar to us. The problem is that not all these habits are in our best interest and our most wicked addiction professes to be our best friends.

Those who are wiser and more fortunate are addicted to good health, prosperity, happiness, positive thinking, and peace of mind. Therefore, they constantly create these things in their lives. Their personalities and their lifestyles demonstrate these good things.

Obvious Addictions

The obvious addicts are those who are addicted to drugs, alcohol, sex, food, gambling, smoking, etc. What they are addicted to is - not loving themselves. They are addicted to pain and punishment, and they bring these addictions to reality by way of their abuses.

Subtle Addictions

The less obvious addicts are those who are addicted to familiarity. They are safe in what is familiar even if what is familiar is bad. Familiar *feels* safer because it is what we know. Unfortunately some things that are familiar to us and to which we become inadvertently addicted are: sadness, anxiety, chaos, rescuing, fixing, worry, misery, people, being right; the list goes on. These are not the more pronounced addictions but they, too, like any other addictions, are detrimental to us and those around us.

Why are we so reluctant to release, move on, detach, separate, or change? Why are we resistant to changing jobs, relationships, habits, opinions or beliefs that are hurting us?

We are reluctant and resistant to change because it is *not* familiar. Change can take us into unfamiliar territory that can be very frightening. Even if we must live with, work, with or regularly interact with people whose behavior is unhealthy or unstable, we know how to cope. We know how to react. We become experts at preparing ourselves and defending ourselves when necessary. We know how to survive. We know how to shut off our feelings and ride out the storms. Familiarity, even if it is bad, feels safer. We who have known unhealthy relationships, which definitely do not feel good, are reluctant to change to healthier relationships because:

1. We don't know anything else or any other way.
2. We don't know what normal or healthy means.
3. We don't know how to function without our difficulties.

Change could take us away from our familiar territory. Change could take us into healthier surroundings. Our need for what is familiar becomes an addiction when we choose what is familiar over what could be healthier.

I am an addict, recovering, but still subconsciously attracting chaos, trouble and anxiety. This is what my whole life has been. This is where I learned to survive. Although I was not truly living but only surviving, I knew nothing else. I did not know things could be different or better.

I am just now becoming aware of my inadvertent attachment to chaos and adversity. I have invited, allowed, enabled, and tolerated these circumstances for as long as I can remember. When my life is hectic or there is a crisis going on, I get right through it. I am the strong one who can keep it together when things are the toughest, but when things start to fall into place when my house is quiet and all is well, my addiction takes over and I create anxiety. I do not consciously want anxiety in my life—it is awful. So now I must learn to live without it. Peace is much healthier, but it feels oh so strange. I simply do not feel as familiar in this calmer more pleasant lifestyle. We must beware for familiarity falsely passes itself off as safer.

Every day I am becoming more aware of my power to create according to my addictions. Some of these addictions put up a tough battle, for they have been a part of me for so long. I am working at overcoming these addictions, but I am not sure I am even aware of all of them.

Yet, I am becoming increasingly confident that they will all be revealed to me as I am ready to conquer them. Small conquests pave the way for larger ones. Each time I resolve one inner conflict, I am more able to beat the next.

If I am to incorporate what I have learned from all the wise books I have read, and if I am to live what I write, then I must use my ability to create according to my desires for a good life. The power to create must be used to supplement my life not feed my addictions. This is an entirely new way, and it is going to take work. I have committed myself to it. It has already paid great dividends. I look forward to reaping greater returns each day.

Throughout the course of writing this book and seeing myself on paper, I have become increasingly aware of my addiction to anxiety. Because of this awareness, I felt less compelled to tolerate it. The impact of becoming aware of my addiction to anxiety smacked me right- square between the eyes. It was quite startling. The acceptance of this realization is helping me to conquer this addiction. It sure has some deep roots. I have to be patient with myself and take my medication.

Addiction to Sad

I am beginning to believe that I subconsciously have the ability to create my own depression and manifest it in the form of a biological depression. The doctor explains otherwise. He explained my biological depression this way. We are intended to be born with a sufficient quantity of chemicals to maintain us throughout our lives, but when we operate on overload for a long time, we deplete our supply and a chemical imbalance is the result. Perhaps some are born with deficiencies.

Yet I am inclined to believe that I contribute to my own depression out of habit. Again, I don't want to do this—depression is awful—but perhaps I do contribute subconsciously. My life was depressing. The people I lived with were depressed; some of them died, and it hurt. That was depressing. Someone was always sick or seriously troubled. Sadness is what I grew up with, and I got hooked. I have no outer condition in my life as I write this; that is depressing, but still I experience depression. My question to myself is: to what degree am I capable of manifesting depression? Psychologically and biologically, what is the cause and what is the effect? Heavy question.

As I look back, I do see a pattern. When there was a crisis in my life, I became strong and stayed in control. As I made conscious decisions and took positive actions to eliminate the unhealthy things in my life, I became oddly uncomfortable. I was always waiting for the other shoe to fall. If no crisis came to me, I conjured one up in my mind. The crisis did not even have to be real. I felt like part of me was missing when there were no problems.

At this point, I cannot tell exactly when I am going to be completely free from these addictions. Still, it is my goal to be free. I believe I have just taken a large step, for I have recognized and identified some serious addictions. These addictions go back a long way and they are very deep, but I found them. Now I can confront them, and ultimately I will take control of them.

I have to express that this has truly been a big revelation to me to see my addictions to anxiety and depression. Again, I don't want them in my life, and the outer circumstances of my life do not reflect this. I no longer attract these conditions outwardly. Now anxiety and depression come from within my body. Is it really possible that I have an unconscious need for them and the ability to create them within myself? Scary question.

Addicted to Rescuing

All my life, I have been a rescuer. I am breaking away from this. I guess it is more accurate to say I am a recovering rescuer.

I believed that God put me on this earth to take care of everyone and everything;, to knock myself out trying to make everything better for everyone. What a *joke*! Here I was going around wiping everyone else's tears, absorbing their pain, then robbing them of the lessons they needed to learn as though my life worked. I'll bet the Lord got a good chuckle out of that one.

I could wipe the tears of others, yet to this day, I am very seldom able to cry. I was so quick and anxious to save others from feeling pain that I was able to ignore my own, and usually, I never really lessened the pain for anyone else. They needed their own pain to grow.

If we are not allowed to feel pain, we will never learn how to process it for ourselves. We will not learn how to develop our own foundation if someone is always trying to rescue us. Sometimes we need to fall, if for no other reason than to learn that we have the ability to get back up. Don't we feel great strength after we have been knocked down, gotten back up, dusted ourselves off, and conquered?

Chapter Nine

Detachment

I first read of detachment in Wayne Dyer's book *You'll See It When You Believe It*. Upon reading of this new thing called detachment, I felt a strange jolt go through me. I knew it was something that I needed to incorporate into Sue. I felt a sense of relief when I first read the word, then I jumped right out of feeling relief into feeling defensive. I, of course, erroneously thought detachment meant withholding love. I was wrong. Detachment demonstrates love for others and love for self.

In my needs and efforts to rescue others, I would try to convey to them how praying has helped me. Talking about praying did not scare them away as I feared it might. I was pleased that they seemed more reassured. But after talking about how much the Lord could and would do for them, I still jumped right in and tried to do everything.

I did things for people that they should have been doing for themselves. I wanted to make their lives easier for them. Of course, it added more hell to my own life, but if I stayed busy enough on my rescue missions, I conveniently did not have the time to look at Sue. This was safer for me.

In my efforts to rescue, not only was I doing obvious things for others that they should have been doing for themselves, but I was also feeling for them and doing their worrying for them. Wasn't I wonderful for doing all these things for them? I would open the way for them to team up with the greatest partner in the universe, then I would politely step right in front of the Lord and take all of these things upon myself. I guess I wanted to make things easier for the Lord too.

Chronic rescuing does not work, but detachment does work. Detachment in the simplest words is the healthiest form of *minding your own business*. It means loving them enough to let them go. It is letting them learn to take responsibility for their own thoughts, beliefs, and actions. It is standing back far enough to see things clearly. It is letting go of the things over which you have no control or have no business having control. It is putting your concerns for them where it belongs—in the hands of God. It is letting go of the neurotic need to get a misery fix.

When we detach, our happiness is no longer contingent upon the happiness or well-being of others. Detachment gives back to each what is rightfully theirs—responsibility for self. When you detach, you will say, "I am okay even if you are not okay. My well-being and my self-worth are independent of your choices. I love you and I will pray for you, but I will not allow your needs and behavior to determine my state of being."

These Subtle Addictions

I remember several years ago when I was talking to a very close friend on the phone. We were commiserating. What problem one of us didn't have, the other did. I was coming to healthier terms with my divorce. I had only been reacting. I was finally at the point to where I was able to take action when I said to this friend, "What am I going to do when I get my life in order? I'll have nothing to talk about. I'll probably go nuts." Well I did follow through and took the necessary actions. I got my life in order—then I cracked up! I did not know how to function without misery and worry.

Progress

I have conquered self-pity—thank goodness. I have given up the rescuing business. I am conquering my own demonic addictions as I recognize them. I have learned to detach, and we are all healthier for it—even Sue. It is up to all the others, whom I needed to rescue, to do their life their way; and it is up to me to let them do it. *And* it is my right and my responsibility to take what the Lord put into this being named Sue, team up with him as my partner, and make Sue all that she is capable of becoming.

Writing about addictions was not part of my original plan. From day one, I have asked the Lord to guide me through this writing project. I am not always sure where he is going to take me, but I am never disappointed. He is opening the craggy doors of those dark places within me. I knew they were in there somewhere, but it was too scary to go near them. Now that the Lord is opening these doors for me, I know that he is guiding me all the way. Therefore, I am not afraid, and his strength enables me to keep my head up and my eyes open. The Lord is distinguishing my friends and foes for me. Oh it is amazing the self-created demons we are conquering. The Lord is helping me to become freer and it *feels good*!

> Don't be afraid, just trust me.
>
> Mark 5:36

Chapter Ten

Examining Me

The happiness of your life depends upon the quality of your thought; therefore, guard accordingly, and take care that you entertain no notions unsuitable to virtue and reasonable nature.

Marcus Aurelius 121–180 AD

How wonderful to be wise,
to understand things,
to be able analyze them
and interpret them.
Wisdom lights up a man's face
softening its hardness.

Ecclesiastes 8:1

As I said earlier, once my thought processes cleared, I had to find Sue. I had to examine my beliefs and my fears, and trace them back to their origin. Our parents, teachers, church leaders, and other people contribute to the development of our belief system.

It is every parent's job to guide their children and teach them right from wrong. Parents do this out of love. The problems occur when our parents' fears are projected into their teachings. They can only teach us what they know, and they can only give to their children what they have inside of them to give.

Therefore, let us not use our parents as scapegoats and blame them for our failures. We are adults now, and to sit back and say, "My parents really screwed me up," is a cop out. Since we are adults now, it is our responsibility to examine our perceptions of their teachings and decide which beliefs are healthy enough for us to keep and which are destructive, and then find the courage to throw them out of our lives.

This is especially hard for me because both my parents are deceased. I can not go back to them and discuss unsettled issues. Since they are both deceased, it seemed incredibly disrespectful for me to criticize them in any way. All I have of them now are the things they showed and taught me. Unfortunately, many of these things are not healthy.

The issues I had with my father were obvious. My father suffered from manic depression, and unfortunately, this occurred at a time when mental illness of any sort was deemed shameful. As a result, no help was available to him. The inner struggle that must have been going on inside him created a living hell for my mother, my sister, my brother, and me. Just looking at him, you knew he was experiencing hell.

I felt it was my responsibility as the oldest child to protect my mother from all threats, harm, and danger. I shielded my sister and brother to the best of my ability. I was too afraid to step between my parents during arguments and never took any action, but I felt such a need to protect her. I needed to protect my father also but did not have a clue how. I diverted my sister and brother from all unpleasantness. The results of my efforts are questionable to this day, for neither of them have much recollection of their childhood. I, on the other hand, remember everything. You can imagine how shameful it is for me to say that when I learned that my father was dead I was relieved. We buried him and no one mentioned him for sixteen years—no questions, no feelings, no nothing.

My Mother

The issues I had with my mother were much more subtle. Only in the last six months have I had the courage to dispute anything I ever heard her say or saw her do. My psychiatrist suggested that I may have unsettled issues with my mother, and I immediately became defensive and protective of her.

Yet somewhere within I knew I had to deal with these issues. So I wrote a list of the things I heard my mother say. This put the responsibility of interpretation on my shoulders and removed any sense of blame from my mother. This was the only way I could do this. In the thirty-two years that we shared, I took everything she said as gospel. The following is a list of the things that I heard my mother say:

- Don't get hurt; get mad.
- People won't like you if you are not nice.
- When we go to visit, don't ask for anything even if you are hungry.
- Don't touch other people's children; they won't like it.
- I don't want to watch you play softball in case you don't hit a home run.
- You should marry a doctor.
- When we drive to the top of this hill, we are going to fall off the world.
- Be tough, don't cry; don't ever cry in public.
- Your laundry isn't clean enough.
- You don't turn your shirts right-way out properly.
- You spoke too loudly and embarrassed me.
- If you would be ashamed to tell me you did something, then don't do it, and if you do, take a gun and shoot me first.
- You can't sleep with two pillows; you don't need one to hug.
- I'm calling the bad school on you, and they will come and get you, and Mrs. Meany will be your teacher.
- Little girls don't wear blue jeans.
- You swing a bat like a girl—swing like a boy.
- The doctor said I have cancer and I can't pray for myself because I am not good enough, so will you pray for me?
- You must be a witch—you are always seeing things and hearing things.
- Only a slut would have a picture of herself kissing her boyfriend. (prom picture)
- You should be somebody.

- You should be the best.
- It's okay if I die because you are strong and you can handle it.
- I wish I could see a psychiatrist.
- Don't start a conversation with people; you might be bothering them.

There you have it, a sampling of the things I heard my mother say. I have to tell you that my mother was also my very best friend. To this day, you will never hear anyone who knew her say an unkind thing about her. She was a wonderful grandmother to my three daughters. We had great fun together, and she did teach me some valuable lessons. There was never a verbal disagreement between us. When she died, I was devastated. I still love her very much. However, I have learned that the things I heard her say were indicative of her own fears and insecurities. I do not hold her responsible for any part of me, for if I did, I would never look into myself. I accepted all she said as gospel. I saw all of her ways as perfect. I incorporated all of her into Sue—I became an extension of her. I knew she loved me and she knew I loved her, but we never said I love you; we never touched.

So when my psychiatrist suggested that I examine my relationship with my mother, I immediately rose to her defense. This wasn't necessary because he was not judging her in any way. I felt if I questioned anything she ever said to me, I would be being disloyal to her. Since she is deceased, I thought I would be attacking my wonderful mother who was not even alive to defend herself. The doctor was sure asking a lot of me. I left his office in an angry and defensive state.

Yet when I got home, I sat right down and wrote the things I heard my mother say. I simply wrote them down. I did not consciously reflect upon them or pick them apart. I tucked them into a file folder.

As I went about my normal routines for the next several days, I became aware that every time I turned a shirt right-way-out, I was doing it the way my mother said I should or I found myself silently apologizing to her for doing it wrong. Still do to this day. Every time I started the washer, I heard that my laundry wasn't clean enough. I also noticed that every time I came near the end of a project I could not finish it. "When we get to the top of the hill, we are going to fall off of the world." What a dumb thing to say to a gullible little kid sitting in the back seat of a car who can't see the road. After all, had she never heard of Christopher Columbus?

After putting the things I heard my mother say in writing, I gradually became aware of the absurdity of some of my beliefs. In examining my beliefs, so many of which were based upon my mother's fears, I finally had to confront her and her death. Although I accepted her death, I had avoided truly coming to candid, frank, blunt, and honest terms with it. I avoided all the feelings that seemed disrespectful and inappropriate. The hardest part for me was to admit my anger and disappointment with her. I needed her to try to be healthy. I needed her to stay alive. I had to deal with the impact of realizing and accepting that she was human too. Doing this was painful, but it has also been freeing and has offered rewards I can't explain.

Most of my beliefs were actually the beliefs of others. I accepted others' beliefs so readily on the surface, that they took root somewhere deep within. Yet there was also a part of me that was rebelling against these beliefs. This rebellion showed itself in the form of trouble. When I relied upon the beliefs of others I was not comfortable, but at least I was loyal. When I projected any of my own beliefs, I was ridiculed, for I was breaking away from beliefs that were passed from generation to generation.

I knew that the time had come to cut the nonsense! All these things I learned and accepted from others for me and me conforming to these beliefs was very limited, insecure, and afraid. *Me* was wasting Sue.

My Father

I then listed the things I heard my father say and the things I saw him do. To do this most effectively, I put myself in the position of a neutral spectator. These are the most memorable things I heard my father say in the fifteen years we spent together.

- If I die, will you miss me?
- I can always count on your curiosity to mess things up.
- Your mother doesn't love me anymore she is a slut.
- Help your mother.
- Your mother doesn't love me anymore, so come into the dark dining room and dance slow (sic) with Daddy.
- The most awful thing I heard my father say was: "Sue bring, me a glass of water." I took a glass of water upstairs to him, and he said, "Now you watch me take all of these pills, and then come lay

> next to me in the dark bedroom until I die." I was thirteen; he didn't die this time.

More than once my mother and us kids were escorted from the house and taken to a park by friends. I was not supposed to know that this was to protect us because my father was allegedly on his way home to kill us.

Often I was aware that he was sitting alone in the kitchen in the dark smoking a cigarette—just sitting. Then suddenly we would hear a glass ashtray crash to pieces against the wall, the door slam, and the car squeal away. My father scared me.

My parents gave me some pretty strong messages. I was an obedient child. I listened to my parents. My parents were all I had as role models. For the first eleven years of my life, they were absolutely everything to me. We very seldom interacted with other families, and our total number of relatives was ten.

I seldom saw my father for he worked two jobs. My mother was always home. Our house was modest but impeccably clean. She made our birthday cakes, sewed our clothes and our doll's clothes. Dinner was the same time every night and there was fresh-baked dessert to go with it.

I only remember two evenings that my mother went out alone. She went to a sewing class. My father watched us. Both times, he asked us if we would miss him if he died, and the second time, he talked to my sister about our long-dead dog until they both cried. I hoped my mother would never leave us with him again.

Church

We sometimes attended church and Sunday school when I was a child. As I grew toward my teens, we drifted away. This was when my parents' marriage got rocky. From what I remember about church, as a child, I perceived the following to be true.

- I would never be worthy of anything, and if I asked God for anything, he would probably say no.
- My sole purpose in life was to raise my children, then I would be of no use—therefore undeserving of life.
- God was always testing me by taking people out of my life.
- I could never measure up enough to make God happy with me; hence, bad things would happen.

Keep in mind that this is not necessarily what was preached in church. The above beliefs came from what I *heard.*

My beliefs were inconsistent and inaccurate, but this was what I knew. Because of my beliefs, I had no confidence in myself whatsoever. I was gullible to flattery and devastated by the slightest criticism. Because I looked to others to find my sense of self-worth, I always came up empty. I was always afraid. You would not have known that by looking at me, for I had to present the image of being in control. It was such a facade. I was a facade and probably more transparent that I would like to think.

I did everything to keep peace. I surrendered my integrity and compromised my intelligence in attempts to soothe the fragile egos of others. This didn't work, but at least I was trying.

I grew to believe that it was terribly wrong to have fun. I believed that having fun caused trouble. So many of the people around me were sick, miserable, angry, and I felt a sense of obligation to deny myself anything pleasurable. I did this out of loyalty to these people and fear of their reactions.

It was so hard to be Sue within my old belief system. I built my belief system to please others. I was wife, mother, daughter, sister, niece, grandchild, student, and employee; and to the best of my knowledge, I did not fail to meet the obligations of these roles. I was good at all of them. Only now do I see that I could have been much more effective in these roles if I had developed my own belief system and defined myself as Sue. I lived to please those I loved and, in doing so, denied Sue. I realize now that if Sue, as she needed to be, had come forth, everyone would have gained.

New Beliefs

Examining Sue and her belief system is the most worthwhile thing I have ever done. It has greatly benefited Sue and those she loves. Being Sue with this new belief system is much easier. Upon examining the old belief system, I have thrown out most of those old beliefs and have since developed much healthier ones. Allow me to give you and example of my healthier beliefs.

- I am responsible for what I choose to believe.
- I need not beat myself up if my old beliefs were wrong or if they have become obsolete.

- I am *not* responsible for my parents' beliefs, words, or actions. I blame them for nothing. I know they love me and did the very best they could for me.
- Although I can never change the things that have happened up to this very moment, I can change the way I think about them.
- God does love me and wants good things for me.
- I am worthwhile.
- I am responsible for Sue, and it is my right and responsibility to allow others to take responsibility for themselves.
- Those that I love are incredibly important to me, but they are gifts from God; and I must acknowledge him before them, for he is the source of their being.
- I can accomplish wonderful things for I know the Lord put me here for ever-unfolding purposes.
- Making Sue the most that she can be according to God's will is a lifelong commitment that is continually bringing Sue more peace and happiness than anything she has ever known.

The first and best victory is to conquer self; to be conquered by self is of all things most shameful and vile.

Plato

Chapter Eleven

Picking Me Apart

In order to examine my belief system and to find which beliefs served a useful purpose, which were of no value, and which were detrimental, I had to pick *me* apart. I would like to offer the following suggestions and guidelines for picking *me* apart. First rule: *Understand that never are you to pick on yourself.* Second rule: *be patient with yourself!* It took years to develop *me*. When picking *me* apart, be as kind, loving, gentle, and encouraging as you would be in teaching your own precious child to walk.

These are some of the rules I used. You may be able to use them as they are or as a guideline in developing your own tools.

What to Look For: Clues to your belief system

The things we heard and saw as we were growing up can greatly influence our current belief system. Think about the things you heard as you grew and tune in to the ones that make the most noise.

Every time I heard _______________, I felt

____

____

Every time I heard _______________, I thought

____

____

Every time I heard _______________, I decided to

____

____

Every time I heard _______________, I

____

____

Every time I saw _______________, I

____

____

Every time I saw ________________, I felt

____

____

Every time I saw________________, I thought

____

____

Every time I saw ________________, I decided to

____

____

Every time I saw ________________, I

____

____

Whenever I feel scared, I

____

____

Whenever I feel neglected, I

____

____

Whenever I feel I am not good enough, I

____

____

Whenever I feel bored, I

____

____

Whenever I feel I am not loved, I

____

____

Whenever I feel loved, I

____

____

Whenever I feel safe, I

____

____

Whenever I feel jealous, I

____

____

Whenever I feel embarrassed, I

____

____

Whenever I feel lonely, I

____

____

Whenever I feel my needs aren't important to others, I

____

____

Whenever I feel I

____

____

The above statements, if completed honestly, will give you clues to your learned responses. Almost all of my reactions were anger and lashing out. I needed to fix this, so then I asked myself: are these responses ones that will help me and my relationships, to grow, or are they detrimental to my growth and my relationships? Also you need to decide if they are your responses or if they are the responses you picked up from others.

Inventory: Cleaning the closet

Examine the things in your life, your mind, your heart. Look in all the corners. Just as in cleaning a closet to put it in a workable order, you may have to do this one layer at a time, or you may just jump right in and scrutinize the whole thing. The goal is to sort through your personal belongings, decide what is valuable and what is not, throw out the junk, save the good stuff, and polish the treasures. Just be patient with yourself and only do as much as you are able to do at one time. As you examine each item, *decide:*

1. *Throw It Out*
   - A. It doesn't work anymore.
   - B. It never did work.
   - C. I don't know how to use it.
   - D. It is dangerous.

2. *Keep It*
   - A. It works.
   - B. It serves a good purpose.
   - C. It helps me to be a better person.

3. *Polish It*
   - A. It helps me to shine.
   - B. It sheds light and helps to inspire.
   - C. It is a demonstration of love.
   - D. It works very well.

4. *Put It into a Box to Sort through Later*
   - A. It is too painful to rationalize right now.
   - B. I need to sort other things first.
   - C. I will test it later to see if it works.

Qualify Each Item

A. Who does it serve?

B. What is its purpose?

C. Will it help me to grow?

D. Will it hold me back?

E. How does it feel in my gut?

F. Does it hurt anyone?

G. Does it work?

Who Is and Who Has Been in My Life

A. How did they get there?

B. Were they invited?

C. Did I invite them?

D. Do I still want them?

E. Do I need them—why or why not?

What about These People

A. Have I hurt any of these people?

B. Can I fix the hurt?

C. Am I willing to fix it?

D. Have any of these people hurt me?

E. Who hurt me and how?

F. Am I willing to forgive them?

G. When I see them or think of them, do my guts feel easy or uneasy?

H. If I find uneasiness, what do I have to do to be rid of it?

What Action Is Required on My Part

A. Forgive
B. Apologize
C. Dismiss
D. Release
E. Ignore

How often are the same types of troubles or are the same troubling circumstances presenting themselves in your life? For years I found myself going from one dysfunctional relationship to another—not limited to male-female relationships, but friendships and work relationships as well. This started long before the word dysfunctional became so popular with therapists.

I always attracted people who demanded unconditional loyalty, who counted on my strength but were also threatened by my strength. If I used my strength to help them in any way, they were happy. But when I used my strength to achieve something constructive for myself, they became threatened and resorted to either physical or emotional abuse. They were always on the verge of going off on a nut!

I told myself that the poor souls needed me. I was a sucker for anyone who had been rejected by others. I believed if I loved them enough and was loyal enough to them, and if I really cared about them, they would be just fine. I thought I could fix them.

Well let me tell you there was a reason others had rejected them. They were difficult people who were looking to others to solve their problems. They were unable to look within themselves and sought suckers like me to nurture their neuroses. To avoid looking within myself, I attached myself to them. Our common denominator was misery. The ironic part is that is was I, *me* who needed to be fixed so that I would not *need* to go around attracting unhealthy relationships, associations, and circumstances. Repeatedly attracting people who needed to be fixed was my subconscious's way of telling me that I needed to be fixed. Too bad I didn't know to listen to my subconscious sooner; it would have saved me a lot of grief.

However, once I listened to what my subconscious was telling me, I put *me* through the examination. I picked *me* apart. I realized that these unhealthy attractions were producing no good fruit. So I went to work on *me*. Now these unhealthy people are just not a part of my life anymore. We are no longer attracted to one another because our common denominator no longer exists. *Hurray!*

We constantly recreate the same type of problems over and over *until* we are able to conquer them. Once conquered, we are free of them forever.

> *Major revelation here: This is how we learn.*

The sooner we learn the lessons we need to learn, the sooner we will stop creating the circumstances that teach us the lesson.

> To stumble twice against the same stone is a proverbial disgrace.
>
> Cicero 106–43 BC

Remember:

1. We create what we need to learn.
2. Until we learn it, we are destined to recreate it.
3. Once we have learned the lesson, we will no longer create the problem.

We need to learn to look and listen to what our lives are showing and telling us. There is a higher consciousness within all of us—call it what you want; I choose the names God, Jesus, Christ, Lord, Love. This higher consciousness truly wants the very best for us. When we don't listen to our higher consciousness, we are bound to keep fumbling, bumbling, and stumbling along. The Lord said, "My yoke is easy and my burden is light … for I am gentle and humble in heart," Matthew 11:29. He is telling us that when we allow him to guide us, he *will* show us a better way. He came to us to be our example. He will show us what really works.

> He who has ears, let him hear.
>
> Matthew 11:15

> So take a new grip on your tired hands, stand firm on your shaky legs, and mark out a straight, smooth path for your feet so that those who follow you, though weak and lame will not fall and hurt themselves, but will become strong.
>
> Hebrews 12:12

Chapter Twelve

Faith or Fear

> Who of you by worrying can add a single hour to his life?
>
> Matthew 6:27

Where there is fear or worry, there is no faith. It's true. Any time that we become worried, we are denying our faith in the Lord. When we worry, we are actually saying, "There is no solution to this problem, even God cannot help." We are in essence telling God that he has no power. Now this is not a good thing to say to the Lord; he probably doesn't like it. And he probably figures that if we don't think he can help, why bother.

When our minds are spinning with worry, they are on overload. Worry consumes us, and very few other things can fit into the mind at this point. If other things do try to get through, we become aggravated. This only compounds the confusion that is a large part of worry. Worry blocks out other things, such as possible solutions. It makes us very tired. Worry lends credence to the word impossible.

Yet we are, in fact, telling God that even he can't help. We become so cluttered with worry/fear that we cannot feel his presence. *We,* through our own absorption of worry/fear, literally block out God's help. Worry/fear closes us up and we aren't even able to let the Lord into our lives. Let me give you an example.

Our youngest daughter, at the time of this writing, was sixteen. She is beautiful and extremely musically gifted. However when she turned fourteen, she was thoroughly convinced that she was the only person who ever had to be fourteen. In her opinion, it was a personal curse. She believed that her older sisters got to the glorious ages of sixteen and eighteen without ever having to experience that agony of being fourteen. She also believed that in your fourteenth year, the number of days in that year was increased from 365 to an infinite number. Fourteen was forever, and she hated it.

This lovely, gifted, intelligent child changed overnight from being a straight-A student to being a certifiably dumb-decision maker. She could no longer tolerate school and skipped and failed. She started running away from home. She attempted suicide. She was diagnosed as manic depressive with suicidal tendencies. She starved herself and carved her own flesh. She spent time in adolescent psychiatric facilities. She ran away some more.

Her behavior and the repercussions of her unhealthy decisions gave us much reason to worry. She was placed on Prozac and did well. Yet she did not like taking Prozac every day.

Two weeks before her sixteenth birthday, we woke up to find her gone again. She left another note. In the note she again berated herself and her foolish behavior and said that she decided she had to leave to get herself straightened out and to keep from causing us any more trouble. We constantly anticipated what she would do next.

In the past when she pulled this, we all went into a frenzy. She usually came home within twenty-four hours. We would talk, she would cry and promise things would get better.

About a week or two before she left this last time, I picked up on her behavior and knew she was going to split again. This time though, instead of worrying myself sick, I gave her to the Lord. I surrendered all of my concerns, my desires for her fate, absolutely all of her to God. I told him that I had done everything I could possibly do for her. I loved her, I never judged her, I clothed her, I hugged her, I fed her, I housed her, I encouraged her, and most important of all, I taught her to pray. I asked the Lord to take control of her. I gave him all my concerns for her. I surrendered everything to God, and this gave me the power of peace. Of course, I did not want to lose her forever, but I honestly felt in my heart that if it was God's will, he would help me.

This time she did not come back home within twenty-four hours. I did not even file a missing-person report with the police until she was missing three days. It may have been unwise, and the police officer did scold me for waiting so long, but I did as I felt guided to do. We followed up on a few leads as to her whereabouts, but I never felt frantic. I was calm in my heart. I felt the Lord's presence constantly. My continual prayer was that the Lord would make his presence know to all of us who were concerned. I prayed that our daughter would feel his presence should she be wise enough to call upon him.

I knew that she would have to be hospitalized again if she returned. She needed psychiatric help. The staff of my two very concerned doctors took care of everything for me. They arranged admission with the psychiatric hospital and the insurance company to the point that all I had to do upon her return was make one phone call. Their blessed assistance was incredibly helpful and comforting. Insurance companies and hospital admission procedures seldom allow for uncomplicated admissions. However, in this case, everything fell right into place.

So the police were notified and admission to the hospital was prearranged, but she did not come home. How do you sleep at night when you don't know where your child is or if she is even alive? When your child is missing, every time the phone rings or someone knocks on the door, you hesitate to answer for fear of bad news. Miraculously I did sleep and function normally. I was able to stave off mental pictures that were based on fear. If worry tried to creep up the back of my neck, I would remind myself that God was in control here and that God was with me, therefore I had peace.

I was also able to go through her room and all of her belongings. I threw away posters, notes, and love letters. I packed up her clothes. I took her bed apart. I didn't cry as I did this. I didn't feel angry, sad, or scared. I only felt strong. I guess the logical part of my mind told me that it would be easier to pack up her things while there was still the hope that she was alive, and if the Lord saw fit to take her to be with him, then this unpleasant task would be done permitting me greater ability to cope.

I am not trying to tell you that I felt absolutely no emotion during this time—quite the contrary. I missed her very much. My love for her remained constant. There were days when I would have fallen to my knees at the sight of her and cried with joy and relief. I could picture myself holding her in my arms. Then there were days when I felt I could have knocked the living daylights out of her for leaving us- for not showing any concern for our love for her.

Time to Detach

This was a time when detachment served me so well. For the first time, I was able dissociate our separate entities. Because I carried her within my body, I felt her to be a part of me. You know, flesh of my flesh. I feel great love for my children, as do most mothers. I devoted all of my time and energy to them. We were on some unexplainable level very connected. We were so connected that, through our behavior, we had the power to significantly affect the feelings of one another. This describes codependency. For clarification, when people are codependent, they base their self-worth and well-being upon the actions and attitudes of others.

When one is free from codependency, he believes and demonstrates the following: "I am a whole person. I have self-worth that is not dependent upon your behavior. I have happiness that is not contingent upon your happiness. I choose to be okay even if you choose not to be okay."

The intensity of our connectedness was not always healthy. When a psychiatrist in charge of her first hospitalization told me that she and I suffered from separation anxiety, I only saw him as cold hearted, and when he made my daughter cry, I signed her out of the hospital AMA. I signed her out against the doctor's advice because I was convinced that I really knew what was best for her. She had cried and told me she really wanted to be okay, that she was tired of trouble, and that she had learned her lessons. I knew all she needed was her mother's love to make her well. Now that she displayed the desire to be good and was listening to me, I knew I could make her fine. So I rescued her from the cold-hearted doctor and took her home and showered her with love.

Guess what? Nothing changed. She still failed school. She still gravitated toward destructive personalities and relationships. She played the lie, cry, promise routine, and I bought it. She still ran the show. We all centered our focus on what she would do next, what kind of mood she was in, whether or not we were making her happy. We allowed her to determine our feelings, our moods, and our actions. She set the tone for the household.

Now a year after I signed her out of the first hospital, she had run away again. As I said earlier, I had sensed that she was wanting to run again. This time instead of going to straighten her out, I went over her head and surrendered all of my concerns for her to God. He certainly did not fail me. He gave me more than I expected. He held my hand, and as I learned later, he also held hers as he helped us to detach from one another.

Through God's help, I was able to let go of her and let her be who she needed to be. I alone could not keep her out of trouble no matter how desperately hard I tried, no matter how much I loved her. I learned that there was no one magic word or phrase that I would eventually say to her that would make her turn her life around. There was no punishment I could give that would instill healthy desires within her. There was no specific thing that I could do. She had to do it for herself and I had to let her—no matter what the cost. If her wants, needs, desires, decisions, and actions caused her to be locked up or dead, I could still do nothing to change her choices.

I could, however, let her fall. I could let her fall hard and leave it to her to turn to the Lord for the strength to get back up. I could continue to pray for her. I could continue to love her. I could continue to encourage her, and I could set an example through my faith. But I could not continue to rescue her from herself. It was time for me to let her go! She had run away again! I hurt! I did feel. But God helped me to stay in control. He helped me not to be ruled by my fears. He showed me his presence and gave me his strength. Therefore, fear never did rule me.

While she was gone, I read the Bible a lot more, especially the Psalms, which are always an incredible source of strength. At one particularly painful time, I asked God to help me find peace for the fears were trying to creep in. I randomly opened the Bible to the forty-sixth Psalm. Verse five says, "God is within her, she will not fall; God will help her at break of day" (NIV). After reading that, I did feel peace. I highlighted the verse and left that particular Bible open to that passage on the coffee table.

Every daybreak, I would wonder if this was the one on which she would return. I waited with faith and trust that the Lord had the entire matter in his very capable hands. I honestly felt his love and peace.

Not knowing if your child, whom you dearly love, is alive or dead is inordinately hard. Without the Lord, I would have cracked. Thankfully though, I didn't crack but took refuge in his strength which he provided in abundance.

Her sixteenth birthday ended without our knowing where she was or if she was alive. That particular night it was extremely cold. Sleet pelted our windows. Fear tempted me. I resisted giving in to such thoughts as was she cold, was she hungry, etc. Instead, I quickly converted the threat of fear to an affirmation of God's loving control.

At about four in the morning after her birthday, the phone rang, and I knew it was news of her. She was being held as a runaway in a police station about fifteen miles from our house. Well, at least I hadn't lost her to death, but when I went to get her, I would have to admit her to the hospital. I still couldn't keep her home.

Many emotions hit me as I saw this skinny, dirty, little girl/nearly-grown woman with tears dripping down her face. I held her and she cried. I took her home, and it was daybreak. She ate and took a shower while I thankfully put her bed back together. It felt good to tuck blankets all around her.

I made the phone call to the admission office at the hospital while she slept. Everything was set for her to be admitted that day. The admission personnel cautioned me that I should bring her to the hospital immediately if she showed any signs of running or harming herself.

When she awoke, we talked. She had bruises and burns on the upper portion of her body. She had carved obscenities into her leg with broken glass. She told me that she had been staying in an abandoned house in the slums of Detroit with no heat and no food. Oh, how I wanted to keep her with me. Thankfully, the Lord gave me the strength to follow through and admit her to the hospital. She admitted that she needed help and agreed to go for a psychiatric evaluation.

At the conclusion of the interview, the doctor advised immediate admission. Up to this point, she was doing very well. When she heard the admission procedures and policies, she started to lose control - immediate admission, no personal belonging, no jewelry, no make up, no phone call, no letters, a shower, and a body search. She became absolutely hysterical and clung to me and pleaded with me to take her home. This child/woman who survived two weeks in an abandoned house in Detroit, this person who never let her family know whether she was alive clutched at me and hurdled promises and threats of suicide. She begged and pleaded with me to take her home. I *hurt*! I was taken by the arm and led to my car, all the time hearing her cries grow fainter with every step I took away from her.

It was so very hard. It hurt so badly. But the Lord gave me the courage to do it. More importantly, he gave me the strength to resist her ploys to be signed out. At every session we had, she made desperate pleas to get signed out. He helped me to look in the face and calmly tell her "I love you, I miss you, and I want you home, but you have to stay here until you are healthy. You have to do this yourself, and I will not take you home before you are ready. The sooner you face yourself honestly, the sooner you will be out." Then I walked away from her again.

To this day, he still gives me the strength to let her take responsibility for herself. All is not perfect at this point, but we are steadily growing healthier. Stepping back and detaching ourselves from each other was a necessary action that we accomplished with love. God carried us through all of this with grace and peace, not necessarily without pain, but certainly not without growth. I shudder to think what the results would have been had we given power to fear instead of faith.

Fear/worry and faith are both enormously powerful. One has the power to build, and the other has the power to destroy. One can never be substituted for the other. They cannot exist in the same place or time, for one always kills the other.

> Then choose for yourselves this day whom you will serve.
>
> Joshua 24:15

Chapter Thirteen

Releasing

So you've come up with all this stuff that serves no one and no useful purpose. What do you do with it. You *release* it! Give it the examination:

- Does is serve anyone or any good purpose?
- Can it be fixed?
- Will someone be hurt more if it is fixed?
- What lessons can be learned from it?

If you have answered no to all the above questions, then I guess you don't need to keep the stuff. What do you do? You *let it go!* If you don't know how to let it go we will discuss that very soon. For now just be *willing.*

Wait a minute. What if you answered yes to any of the above questions?

- If it serves a purpose, take from it that which serves and let the rest go.
- If it serves someone, give the useful part to them and let the rest go.
- If it can be fixed, fix it now.
- If no one will be hurt by it, make amends, and then let the rest go.
- If it has taught you a lesson, learn the lesson. Store it in your *book of knowledge* for future reference and let the rest go.

Guilt is the teacher, and our conscience is the head master. It is guilt's job to teach us. It is our conscious responsibility to learn the lesson. After the lesson is learned, guilt serves no purpose.

If you choose to carry around worthless guilt, you are denying a lesson. The sooner you master the lesson, the sooner the bedeviling guilt will leave you. Process it and put it where it belongs.

We all make mistakes. This is how we learn and grow. Put all your mistakes to work for you. You process them and they will not control you. We all create mistakes as learning tools. It is part of being human and, it is the reason we are on earth.

We were not meant to be perfect, and there are at least two substantial reasons for this:

1. We are here to learn and grow. Without the lessons of mistakes, we would never grow.
2. If we were perfect, we would not need God.

So take it easy on yourself. Always strive to do your best. If you fall short, process it, examine it, fix it. Fix it *now* if doing so will cause no further harm. Make amends and restitution if necessary. Above all, ask the Lord to guide you. You'll know you're on the right track when your gut feels peace.

To make a mistake is not a sin. To repeat mistakes and never fix this or learn from them is a sin against oneself and a waste of a life.

Forgiving

The grudges that we hold against one another or against ourselves are like a cancer. They eat away at us.

I've come across more people whose energy is spent on plotting some type of revenge. They constantly feel the need to get even. They are like time bombs waiting to go off. Only problem is that should the bomb go off, it usually explodes in the face of the wrong person.

Raising my three daughters through their teenage years prompted the necessity for my husband and me to diffuse more than one hostile situation: an angry boyfriend who was going to kick someone's butt, the jealous one who was going to tell so and so this or that.

These kids were thriving on their animosities. They nurtured their hostilities and they grew. More friends became involved, and before long, we literally had wars going on, with threatening phone calls, damage to cars, ultimately a public attack/assault/confrontations in which absolutely no one gained a thing—except the lawyers.

Forgiveness is a prerequisite to releasing. Until not too

long ago, I had a difficult time understanding the criterion and the power of forgiveness. Consequently, I could not totally forgive. Let me attempt to explain forgiveness as I have come to understand it. First, let us ascertain what forgiveness does *not* mean.

Forgiveness Does Not Mean:

1. You have to like the person.
2. You have to condone their behavior.
3. You have to agree with their beliefs.
4. You have to continue to abide or associate with them.
5. You have to be their doormat or their punching bag.
6. You have to be a victim.

Forgiveness Does Mean:

1. You recognize that God is also within that person even though that person may not behave in a way that demonstrates his indwelling God.
2. You bypass the person and go straight to their God within, for it is the same God that is within you.
3. You acknowledge their indwelling God and tell God that you want peace with this person. You accept that the other person is only doing what he knows how to do at this time.
4. You ask God to guide that person along.
5. You ask God to assist you in detaching from their behavior.
6. You ask Got to make his presence known should the two of you meet again.
7. You ask the Lord to bless that person as he sees fit.

To test this process, think of that person. When forgiveness has taken place, there is positively no feeling of animosity. There is only a feeling of peace and a sense of healthy separation.

We keep ourselves connected to people we don't like because we fail to forgive them. They probably don't want to be around us any more than we want to be around them. Yet, because we have not forgiven them, they and the unhealthy feelings and behaviors they represent continue to exist and interfere.

When forgiveness is achieved, all those nasty feelings give way to a feeling of peace or just a feeling of comfortable neutrality. The burden is now off you. You feel so much lighter and freer. It is wonderful! You don't need those nasty feelings; they don't make anything better. Total forgiveness is what it takes and it really works.

The List

One day I made a list of every person that I could ever remember being in my life. As I wrote down their names, I paid attention to what I felt. I briefly felt the emotions that I had attached to that person and made a short note next to their name.

Then I went over the list slowly and thoroughly. I did not have the time to do this all at once, but once I started the process, I went to it daily until I had gotten through the entire list. What a therapeutic endeavor this turned out to be.

As I came upon each person's name, I brought him/her into my mind and felt what they represented. I processed the feelings completely. I thought of the timid girl that I was mean to in the fourth grade. I was mean to her just because I didn't like the way she looked. She had dark curly hair and freckles. So did I. I also didn't like the way I looked. Anyway, I brought her into my mind and greeted her. *Hi, Sharon. I was very mean to you in the fourth grade, and I am very sorry. Please forgive me. God bless you. Good-bye, Sharon.* Then I moved on to the next person on the list.

Perhaps the name on the list would represent someone who treated me wonderfully. I enjoyed the good feelings I felt, greeted the person, told them why I cared about them, thanked them, and asked God to bless them. Then I moved on.

Others stirred up some very painful feelings. Again, I greeted the person in my mind. I told them how I felt without blame or desire for revenge. I told them how their behavior or actions distressed me then and now. I told them that I forgave them. I acknowledged their indwelling God and asked his blessing upon them. I moved on.

By the time I finished this list, I was well on my way to becoming a different person—a freer person, a healthier person, and a much happier person. I was no longer burdened with cumbersome worries or fears. I had cleansed my memory. I had cleared out a whole bunch of space. I had more energy because my thoughts no longer weighed me down. I had more patience and understanding.

Serenity Prayer

The Serenity Prayer is extraordinarily useful in achieving forgiveness. Let the essence of the Serenity Prayer rule as you do your list. Think of it this way:

> God, you and I both know that what has happened in the past cannot be changed, so please grant me

> your peace in accepting these matters. God, we know that the only thing that can be changed is our feelings, our attitudes and our reactions to what has happened. Please grant us your strength in rising above the pain. Help us to convert our pain to your peace. God, I constantly seek your wisdom in all that I think, feel, say and do. Amen
>
> Alcoholic's Anonymous paraphrased

Is Forgiveness Needed?

Somewhere along the way, I read something regarding forgiveness that has proven to be very valuable. I cannot remember where I read it; therefore, I cannot give proper credit. I will paraphrase as best I can.

If, when you are praying the Lord's Prayer, your mind starts to wander about the time you come to the part that says "forgive us our debts," this indicates a need for forgiveness somewhere. Ask the Lord to help you find it.

This was most useful to me because every time I prayed the Lord's Prayer and I got to the forgive part; sure enough, my mind would start to wander. The trouble is I didn't pay attention to where it wandered. I just sort of drifted off—somewhere. After reading that, this is an indication of the need for forgiveness, I started to pay attention to where my mind wandered. Sure enough, I found my mind eventually thinking of someone or something that needed to be forgiven or fixed.

Resistance to Releasing

Sometimes things are so deeply ingrained within us that we just cannot see them clearly. Attached to these deeply rooted feeling may be an unconscious resistance to letting these thing go. At the risk of sounding corny or superstitious, I always ask God to help me release any hidden resistance to forgiving and releasing. In doing this, I often have thoughts come to me out of the blue that give me some valuable insight to something that has been stuck within for a long time. Because of this insight, I am better able to put this thing into its proper perspective.

So How Do You Release?

Just about everything I have read, including the Bible, encourages us to shift from what is negative to what is positive. We are encouraged to get rid of the junk and let God fill us with good stuff. We know that releasing is necessary, yet I have often heard myself and others give a resounding "*How?*"

The answer came to me while I was participating in the parent-support group held in conjunction with my daughter's last hospitalization. As I sat with this group and looked around, I saw that familiar anguish reflected on the face's of other parents. I definitely had felt that same anguish too often and it was dreadful. You feel so helpless and so very, very tired. Still, deep within me, I did not feel what their faces reflected. I felt peace. I am not saying that I did not learn anything from the parent-support group, but because I had placed everything in the hands of the Lord, I was able to experience peace. I knew that I could handle whatever happened from that moment because God was working within me.

This immense peace did not place me above the other parents in any way. I could relate to and understand all they felt. Acknowledgment of our higher consciousness was a large part of the program. I tried my very best to convey to these parents the need to surrender their worries to their higher consciousness. Some were just not ready.

One woman seemed to stand out more than the rest. Perhaps she was more vocal about her pain. This woman, bless her heart, was existing in vicious cycle of hate, blame, anger, resentment, and the need to retaliate. She was figuratively paralyzed, and she was hurting. Her presence screamed pain.

My heart went out to her. After one parent session, I went home and went to bed. I was just lying there sort of drifting and sharing my thoughts with God. This woman with her excruciating pain and volatile anger came into my mind, and I clearly saw the following in the form of a mental movie. It is difficult to explain what I call a mental movie. These movies are what my mother was referring to when she said I saw things. Not only do I see the movie, I also feel it. I will describe it as I experienced it.

White Doves and Black Satin

I saw the words *white doves and black satin*. I experienced myself sitting on the floor during a parent-support session with this woman's head cradled in my lap. She was rigid with pain and anger. As I gently stroked her head, she appeared to become calmer. I said the following things to her in a very soothing voice.

"It is okay; you are not alone. We see your pain and we feel it too, but you don't need all of this pain." I asked her if she was willing to let go of her pain and anger. Very weakly, she nodded yes. "Okay, just close your eyes and know that you are not alone and that you are loved. See yourself in your mind. See yourself spreading out a large brand new piece of black-satin cloth on the floor. Make sure it is smooth with no wrinkles. Now see yourself in front of the black satin. You are very comfortable and very safe. Now bring up the pain, and as it comes to you, take it from yourself and place it on the black satin. See each pain as an object, physically remove it from yourself, and place it on the black satin.

"Take all the pain you associate with your father, and place it on the black satin. Do you see the pain and anger you felt when your father ignored you as a child? Do you feel the pain and the abuse? Gather up all the pain, anger, resentment, and hate; take it from yourself; and put it on the black satin. All pain associated with your father is now out of you and on the black satin.

"Now gather all the pain, humiliation, degradation that you experienced with your ex-husband. Take out all the anger, hate, animosity, and need for revenge that you have carried for years. Take out each parcel, and put it on the black satin.

"Now find all of your fears, worries, and concerns for your daughter. Be sure you have all of them. Find the rejection you feel when she runs. Find the fear you experience when you don't know where she is or what she is doing. Go in and get the false beliefs that you have not been a good mother. Take your mistakes and bundle them up too. Take all these feelings and concerns for your daughter and your relationship with her and place every one of them on the black satin.

"Now go in and find all the miscellaneous remnants of

pain, disappointment, jealousy, blame, fear, worry, and any other nasty stuff you can find, and place it on the black satin.

"You have carefully checked all the dark places within you, and you have taken all the bad things out of yourself, and they are now in front of you on the black satin. Once they are on the black satin, they cannot come back into you."

As I continued to stroke her head and speak to her, we could all see peace moving in.

I then said to her, "Now that you have all of this pain out of you, it cannot come back. You have placed it on the black satin, and you are ready to send it away forever.

"Look to the sky and feel the love of the Lord. Feel it enfold you. You are safe and you are protected. From the sky, on shimmering planes of light, you see four beautiful doves descending. The closer they come, the safer you feel. These doves are God's couriers of love and peace. One dove settles on each corner of the black satin. Carefully they grasp the corners of the satin. Securely holding the corners of the black satin, they ascend toward the heavens. All of the pain and sorrow you placed on the black satin is being carried far away from you by the doves. The doves are luminescent. They shimmer. They radiate waves of love and peace. Although you can still see the doves, they have carried your black satin parcel of pain high into the heavens where they suddenly fly off in four different directions causing the black satin to fling all of your pain to the heavens where God, in his love for you, converts all of this pain into light. Healing, soothing, twinkling, sparkling, dazzling lights fall back down onto you. Every hole and every space that was created when you removed the pain is now filled with the healing loving light of the Lord. You are whole. You are loved, and you are safe; you are never alone, and you can call upon the white doves any time you feel the need. They will always come. They will carry your pain to the heavens where it is abolished and obliterated, where it is converted to the healing light of God's love. This light always returns to you to fill the voids. Where there was pain there is now peace."

Then abruptly my mental movie was over. It was like waking from a dream, but I had not been asleep. I had become so engrossed and totally absorbed in this mental movie that I was quite startled when it was over.

Visualization

Visualization was the answer to that resounding *how*. Visualization provides the means for releasing. I tried it for myself. I used the white doves and black satin technique. I had previously identified several parcels of junk that I no longer wanted to carry around, yet they still lurked about.

So I replayed my mental movie, but this time with my head being stroked by angels. In my own mental movie, they spoke to me and guided me. *It worked!* What peace I felt. That peace is still with me. Finally, I had peace where there had been pain.

I never did present this at the parent group. Our daughter was discharged several days later and we no longer participated in the group. About three months later, my husband and I saw this woman at her place of work. She was busy assisting someone and did not see us. We did stand off to the side hoping to speak with her, but she stayed busy and we had to leave.

My husband and I could not help but notice that she appeared to be extremely exhausted and haggard. Again, my heart went out to her. Perhaps one day she will read this—maybe it will help—in the mean time she is in my prayers.

Other Visualization Techniques

My brother-in-law was one voice in that resounding *how*. We were having a discussion about the dumb things we hold onto and how they hold us back. His question was, "I know I don't need this stuff, but how do I get rid of it?" I attempted to describe the white doves and black satin to him, but I rushed through it, and he only responded with a look that indicated he thought I was off my rocker. Seeing this quizzical look on his face, I backed up a step and tried to explain to him how we could use visualization as a means of releasing.

Then I thought perhaps he could relate to a more masculine form of visualization. So I suggested that he identify his mental junk, pack it up, put it on his truck and dump it over a cliff. I told him to see his troubles leaving him and falling over a cliff. However, his face still revealed skepticism, but I did see a glint in his eye that I immediately hoped was at least a vague understanding of what I was saying.

Pop-up Carnival Critters

Okay, you just read the three words above and are probably thinking like my brother-in-law that I am indeed off my rocker. Don't give up on me yet, please.

When things start to get to me and I feel the walls closing in, I need to escape. My most effective escape is to go to my room and stretch out on my bed. I get cozy and comfortable and visit with God. Then I just sort of drift and see where my mind or my imagination takes me. Sometimes I fall asleep. Otherwise, I daydream. Often I do some much-needed mental house cleaning. This time of relaxation shared with God is a very refreshing time for me. It revitalizes me.

I have always had a difficult time sleeping at night. I remember this difficulty as a child, and if my dear mother were still here, she would attest to that fact, for she resorted to extreme measures to get me to sleep as an infant. Sometimes she would throw me into the car and drive around until I fell asleep and then creep back into the house and put me to bed. Another trick she resorted to was to lie on her back on the floor under my crib, grab a hold of the springs, and rock—more accurately shake—the crib until I fell asleep. Bless her heart!

Most often, the anxiety attacks that plague me occur at night when I try to sleep. Instead of lying down at night and unwinding, my mind starts to race. I become very restless, and it is as though thousands of little voices are screaming my weaknesses, my fears, and my shortcomings at me. I feel the need to run.

One afternoon during a drifting period, I saw another mental movie. I could see and feel myself running from these vicious little voices. Suddenly I saw myself *stop* and *turn* and *confront* the voices that were chasing me.

I faced them with my hands firmly on my hips. They taunted me. I can only liken the visual image of the voices to a game I used to play at a carnival when I was a kid. When you played this game, you were given a rubber mallet. In front of you was a counter that was full of uniform holes about two to three inches in diameter. Your job as the player in the game was to watch the holes, out of which popped little gopher-like critters. They popped quickly and randomly up and down, in and out of their little holes. The object of the game was to belt these little critters with the rubber mallet before they went back down into their holes. The more critters you belted, the higher your score.

In my mental movie, I saw myself stop and turn and face them. I confronted them. They, just like the carnival critters, popped up and down jeering and hurling taunts at me. I looked and saw I was armed with a rubber mallet. I felt empowered. I called out to these savage critter voices, "All right, I'm ready. Just try to get me." One popped up and in a sing-song voice screamed, "Nobody loves you." *Whap!* I belted him with the mallet, and he was gone. Another popped up and professed in that same annoying sing-song voice, "You're going to fail." I belted the living daylights out of that one, and he was gone. "Ha, ha, ha, ha, ha, ha, you're really dumb," sang another. I pulverized him. More popped up and taunted me. One by one, I clobbered them with my rubber mallet until there was just silence. It was great! I loved it!

If all of this sounds corny to you, then perhaps my imagination is just a little more eccentric than yours. This does not make either of us wrong.

Visualization is an extremely effective tool. So when you are ready to stop carrying around all that useless junk, pack it up and see yourself discarding it forever in any fashion that suits your imagination. This will create space for better things.

Chapter Fourteen

The Voids

There can be no voids. When something leaves or goes away, it leaves a space—a void. I believe that Jesus was making this point in the eleventh chapter of Luke, verses 24–26. Here he speaks of a demon leaving a man. The place that the demon left is now clean. The demon tries to come back to that clean place, and it comes back with seven demons more wicked than itself to fill that space. The point: the place will not stay empty. The lesson: fill the space with something good, or evil will come back and fill it.

Let us take care of the spaces we create when we throw out our junk. We must guard that something as bad or worse does not takes its place. Therefore, the visualization process of throwing your mental garbage to the heavens for transformation to light to fill the voids takes more meaning. No things and no persons can fill those spaces with anything better than God. If something unlike God, hence something not good, fills those clean spaces we are destined for more trouble.

Other Voids

Many of us get ourselves into trouble because we feel empty. We feel there is something missing in our lives. Perhaps we feel lack of self-confidence. When we are forced to face a situation that calls for confidence, we grab the closest thing to it that we can find. This may be another person to handle the situation. This may be liquid courage in the form of alcohol. This may be a numbing of the senses through the use of drugs. But because we lack self-confidence, never do we look within ourselves to our higher consciousness for the confidence we lack. We sense a void and fill it with anything that will pull us through—this time.

The last place we look for confidence is within ourselves. Yet it can be found nowhere else. If we want to test this theory, we can do the following.

When a difficult circumstance arises and we feel inadequate to speak or to act, we say a prayer to our Lord within instead of looking outside of ourselves. When we ask the Lord to speak and act through us, and trust that he will—confidence is ours. We say a prayer. We take a deep breath. As we take that deep breath, we feel the strength we need fill us just as the air fills our lungs. We have to learn to always look within. God is there.

Voids in Relationships

Seldom are voids more apparent and potentially damaging than in our personal relationships. We get into an intimate relationship. For a while, we float around. We are ecstatic and radiant. The excitement of a promising new relationship sets us aglow. Gradually the newness wears off and we again become aware of that nagging emptiness. Then we run the gamut. The questions start. What is the matter with me? What is the matter with you? Don't you love me anymore? Why don't you care about me the way you used to? On and on. I'm sure you get the picture. Most of us, at one time or another have probably been part of a similar scenario.

Regardless of the individual circumstances, the relationship is no longer new and exciting. It is empty and troubled. Some stay with the relationship until they have beaten it into the ground. Some hang onto the empty relationship only for a specific convenience. Others bail out and find another new and promising relationship that ultimately ends up the same way.

I looked to others to fill this miserable emptiness. I know plenty of others have done so too. I know their stories—different names and places, otherwise, same story. My husband is a remarkably wonderful man. Yet I nearly sabotaged our relationship when I perceived him as "my everything." I put him before the source of his being. I looked to him for utter fulfillment. My sense of well-being, my happiness, and my success was in every way contingent upon him. I held him responsible for me.

He never volunteered for this dubious honor. I bestowed it upon him, and boy, did I raise a fuss when he fell short of my expectations. Whenever that emptiness approached,

I blamed him. I honestly felt he was failing me, and yet I believed he was failing me because he was mean. Of course, anger was my automatic recourse, and I wanted to make this guy pay! This was all I knew. This was how my life and relationships had always operated.

This potentially wonderful relationship was one step away from ruin. At some point during this rocky period, my husband said to me, "Don't you have any faith in me yet?"

I had heard those words before and they rang loud as a bell. Jesus said these same words in Mark 4:40. Again, it was necessary for me to surrender my ways and old habits to God. I prayed for the Lord's guidance and asked him to let me feel what he would have me feel. I asked him to give me the strength to do what he would have me do. Once more, he did not fail me.

It was about this time that I was placed on Prozac, which helped immensely. Once I regained control of my thoughts and attained the ability to place things into a rational perspective, I had to do some serious soul searching. I had to examine my beliefs and confront my fears.

Thankfully, through God's grace, my husband, Ken, and I have been blessed with the ability to communicate effectively. We began to share our fears openly and honestly. We started this sharing slowly and cautiously. It grew. This brought real magic to our relationship, for it was founded on a mutual trust and respect.

We began to see what reality meant. We stopped throwing curves at one another, and we stopped asking trick questions. When a question that seemed trivial or asinine came up, we learned to take the time to figure out where it was really coming from. What old hurt was coming through? When we sought its origin, we usually found some old fear or the unpleasant remains of past hurts. We identified the real fear and explained it as best we could. This enabled us to truly understand one another and offer sincere reassurance. We made it a practice to say what we really meant and to ask specifically what we wanted to know. This has now become a habit. This works. Our relationship has surpassed the joy we hoped for when the relationship was new.

It is true. In order to have a healthy relationship with another person, you must first establish a healthy relationship with God and yourself—in that order. Nothing else works. I fired my husband from the prominent position of "my everything" and hired God. Good help isn't so hard to find, just take one of the *o*'s out of good.

Chapter Fifteen

The Transition

At this point, let's recap. We understand that our physical, mental, and spiritual attributes form a complete circle. We have had our medical physicals. We have discussed and identified endogenous depression and anxiety disorder as a major roadblock to a workable life. Remember it is imperative that this is not overlooked or taken lightly. It is a real disease that causes you not to work properly. It can happen to anyone. Apparently, constant stress can contribute to this disorder. These days stress seems to be our most abundant commodity. Therefore, a biological depression must be treated or ruled out *first*.

We have dissected anger. We know that it has its place, but we also know that it disguises itself as our loyal protector.

We know that anger can cover our true feelings and allows us the false security of staying stuck. Putting anger in its proper place grants us the freedom to be honest with ourselves and to be straight with others.

We have examined our belief systems and determined which beliefs we choose for ourselves and those we have adopted from others. We have weeded out the beliefs that hold us back and serve no useful purpose. We have replaced these restrictive beliefs with ones that encourage us to become increasingly aware of our unlimited potentials. We accept the lifelong commitment of keeping our beliefs in check.

We have *looked deep within ourselves* to find of what we are made. We should be extremely proud of ourselves, for in doing this, we have demonstrated courage. We realize that we are far more than physical entities. We have captured the ability to get ourselves *unstuck.*

We know that when something leaves us, something must take its place. There can be no *voids*. We are careful to be sure that the new things that come to us, as the old things leave us, are healthier and constitute continued growth.

We know the value of *surrendering*. This is what truly gives us our power. We have the ability and the right to empower ourselves in any and every situation.

We know that *faith* and *fear* cannot coexist. We understand that they are both very powerful forces and that one *always* destroys the other. Where there is fear there is no faith. And where there is faith there is no fear.

We know the healthy merits of *forgiving and releasing:* when we forgive and release, we enable ourselves to stop our mental conversations and arguments and know peace. We are able to trust that through forgiveness and releasing our thoughts, feelings, words, and deeds, we will be guided by the Lord in any given situation if we look to him *first*.

We know that *we are not alone*, that our higher power, our God, is within us. He is always within us. And it is up to us to turn to him. This is called *choice*.

We all recognize our desire for freedom. It is inherent. We must remember though that we, ourselves, are the ones who deny our own freedom. We keep ourselves prisoners. Is it not time to free ourselves? Is it really too soon to *really live*?

> Then you will know the truth, and the truth will set you free.
>
> John 8:32

Now that we have cleansed our souls, so to speak, it is time to take the big step. It is time for us to transcend from our lower selves, where we are limited, to our higher selves where we are free and able to grow into all the Lord intended us to be. This transition is never to be thought of as temporary. Although as we grow into the consciousness, we may slip back now and then, we know that this transition is perpetual. We know that we are always capable of higher growth. When we truly want to really live our lives, we will make a conscious decision to adopt a new focus. This focus is tuning in our God in all that we think, feel, do, and say. This is not tedious or difficult; it is so much *easier*. The more we do this, the stronger we grow, and the more we are able to do.

We no longer need to spin in endless circles. We don't need frustration. We don't have to make everything difficult.

There is no greater gift we can give to ourselves and to others than to make this transition into our higher selves.

Jesus promises us that his way is easier for in Matthew 11:29–30. He encourages us by saying, "Take my yoke upon you and learn from me, for I am gentle and humble in heart, and you will find rest for your souls. For my yoke is easy and my burden is light."

Jesus also promises us in John 10:10 that he has come that "we may have life and have it to the full."

I have learned that the teachings of Jesus, as I have come to understand them, give true peace and real meaning to my life. Nothing has worked as well as the Lord. As I have stated before, I do not belong to any one organized religion. I am far from perfect; I am probably a lot like you. I want to do good things and I want to enjoy my life. I make mistakes and I stumble and often fall short of the mark. Like you, I need to love and be loved. I need to respect and to be respected. I need to express myself and I need to *be.*

I guess we are all pretty much alike. We learn through trial and error. I have learned through much trial and error that my way alone is difficult, limited, and frustrating. I have learned that when I listen to what Jesus taught us, my life is easier and it works much better. For the wonderful thing that I have learned is that *whatever* I need, *whenever* I need it, the Lord is more than willing to give it to me if I ask him from my heart and let him help in his way.

Chapter Sixteen

The Ways of Man Opposed to the Ways of God

Let us be thankful for all the wonderful human beings who have made great contributions to this world, those who have used their talents to make this world a better place. There are indeed many of them. Yet just the smallest bit of attention to the media on any given day will cause us to become sadly aware that people love dirt. It is the sorry state of the world that receives the most publicity and opposes all that God gave us, all that God is, and what Jesus came to exemplify. This sorry state of opposition to God is the topic of this chapter.

If you still have any reservations about putting all of yourself in to the care of God and his will, let us consider and compare the ways of man to the ways of God. I am using the term "man" to refer to all of humanity throughout history.

What God Has Created

1. The universe, vast and unlimited
2. Abundant earth
3. Regeneration and reproduction
4. Food, water, plants, and animals
5. Man/woman

What God Has Given to Man

1. Dominion over all
2. Earth rich with resources
3. The ability to reason thereby create
4. The ability to choose how to use God's resources thereby the ability to create his own destiny
5. The ability to think good or evil
6. Everything man needs in abundance—God held nothing back

> But whatever is good and perfect comes to us from God.
>
> James 1:17

What God's Gifts Can Show Us

God gave us everything good. If we take the time to look at nature, we can learn many things. If we look at these things constructively and observe them in their most simple forms, perhaps we can apply the basic principles of their existence to our lives. When God provided us with all the gifts of nature, he gave us much more than a means for survival. When we become aware of his *wondrous* gifts, we can see that he also gave some wonderful lessons and examples.

> But ask the animals, and they will teach you, or the birds of the air, they will tell you; or speak to the earth, and it will teach you, or let the fish of the sea inform you. Which of these does not know that the hand of the Lord has done this. In his hand is the life of every creature and the breath of all mankind.
>
> Job 12:7–10

What Plants Can Show Us

Consider everything that grows from the earth—trees, flowers, food, bushes, etc. Consider what these things can show us. All they really require to exist is soil, water, and sun. Their quality can be enhanced with fertilizing, pruning, and nurturing. They have within their own being all they require to be beautiful, to grow, to serve a purpose, to reproduce. They cannot do anything for themselves except grow, thrive, produce, or die. They are at the mercy of elements and man.

Consider what the flowers in the field can show us. For the time that they are on this earth, they are glorious. They dance in the breeze, they shimmer with dew in the sun, and they grow stronger when the rain falls upon them. When their time is done, they leave seeds. These seeds fall to the soil or are carried by the wind to other places. These seeds must dry and appear to be lifeless before they can grow anew. The natural tendency of plants is ever-life-sustaining. Can you see the lessons?

What Animals Can Show Us

Animals can be our teachers. Of course they provide food for us, but there is much more. There is such an enormous number of species, each with its own characteristics and purpose. One characteristic that is common is that when the animals are not threatened or controlled, they are extremely playful. Playfulness is an instinct, and there are few things more innocently pleasurable than watching animals at play. Also there are few sights more savagely ugly than to see animals killing and feeding off one another.

Animals will kill to protect their young, but they also instinctively know when it is time to let their young fend for themselves.

The Earth and the Universe

The earth just keeps spinning in the heavens. It has no apparent choice. Short of blowing it out of the heavens, man cannot stop the movement of the earth. What comes from the earth? An abundance of jewels, energy, and raw materials. These things are not scarce. Man may waste them and cause a threat of shortage, but they are supplied in great abundance. Scarcity is not the way of nature.

The skies are endless. The components of the solar system are incomprehensibly enormous. On a clear night you can sit anywhere and see the Big Dipper. Even though we may travel thousands of miles, the Big Dipper is still right above us. Incredible! Look to the skies. There are wonders in every direction. These wonders are constant. They are always there. There are no limits. *There is no end.*

Imagine man without the curse of ego. Imagine that he cannot make any decisions that serve just himself—that everything true that is demonstrated in the life-sustaining tendencies of nature is true of man. Think about it. Would we not see that it is natural for us to play, to protect our young, to release them when the time is right, to cease to worry, to cease to struggle for power, to realize that we are life-sustaining? Would we not see that we are unique? We are all beautiful in our own way. We have our own purpose. We serve a useful function; there is a power or force greater than us. There are no limits; there is no end.

The characteristics that are only of man are the cause of what man chooses. Man and his ego are the downfall of man. Think about that.

Perhaps it would serve us well to incorporate more of the ways of nature into our own existence—placing more emphasis on what is natural and life-sustaining and placing less emphasis on the false and deceptive rewards that man's ego seeks.

Balance

This world is out of balance. The major emphasis is placed on self serving self; hence dominance by ego. Perhaps if the emphasis was on a self that first served God, balance would be achieved. God did a fine job of balancing the universe, the earth, the animal kingdom, horticulture, the human body itself; no man could possibly create the intricacies of the universe from the unknown expanse of the heavens to the proficiency with which a cell reproduces itself. Man has thrown the physical and the spiritual aspects of God's creations out of balance. God knows what we need, and he is willing to give it to us.

> Your heavenly Father knows you need them. But seek first his kingdom and his righteousness, and all these things will be given to you as well.
>
> Matthew 6:32–33

Are we not foolish to overlook all that the Lord gave us and realize that he is more than capable of creating within each individual a specific beauty, purpose, and a distinct uniqueness that can only be proclaimed a *wonder*?

What Man Has Done with God's Gifts

Man Has:

1. Allowed greed to hurt others
2. Used energy to harm
3. Used pride to deny God
4. Created danger for himself and all humans through the abuse of energy and the need/quest for personal power and glory
5. Neglected the responsibilities to his own soul in his need to dominate others

Man has even created wars, death, and destruction to demonstrate his interpretation of God and to force his interpretations upon others. Man has the audacity to destroy in the name of God.

> Trust in the Lord with all your heart and lean not on

> your own understanding; in all your ways acknowledge him, and he will make your paths straight.
>
> Proverbs 3:5–6

God the Parent

What it must be for God the Parent to watch his children destroy. How utterly painful and discouraging it is for any parent to give everything to his child so the child can have everything and to realize that the child doesn't appreciate it—he just wants more—never taking the time to thank the parent for what he does have. The child misuses the gifts and all the children suffer for it. The parent must be sad.

As parents we know the pain of watching our own children make unhealthy decisions, choose destructive paths, and run from one crisis to the next. As parents we have experienced the anguish of watching a wayward child struggle. We know that we can help and guide that child if only he/she would let us. We feel our children's pain, but so often we are helpless and/or powerless to help them because they won't let us.

How many children does God the Parent have? Some of his children are a great source of joy. Sadly though, more are a source of pain. Just take note of what the media has to say about the condition of the world today. It isn't very encouraging.

God the Parent must cry for his children who do not or will not love or respect him. Some publicly denounce him, and some openly ridicule him and all that he stands for.

Isn't it wonderful that God isn't codependent? Isn't it really in our best interest that God, our Parent, allows us the freedom to make our choices? God gave us an example of perfect life when he came to us as Christ. God's glory is not dependent upon the behavior of his children. He lets us fall. Sometimes he lets us fall hard. Since his glory is independent of the actions of his children, he never falters. He always works perfectly. And when he sees that we come to him openly, he picks us up and puts us on the right track. It is a shame that God's children don't trust that he is so willing to give. It is too easy for us to disregard the accessibility of the unlimited and wonderful gifts of God. Why don't we see?

God has shown us that there are no limits to what he will give us. The abundance of nature clearly demonstrates this. Yet, too many of God's children don't even see these things. Their view of these things is obscured by greed, selfishness, and the wallowing in their self-created pain, to which they give all power and glory.

Greed, selfishness, and pain deserve no glory. Yet we put these things on display for all to admire and we are devastated when these things bring no glory back to us. Then we have the audacity to pout about it, indulge in self-pity, or worse yet, blame God.

We are responsible for giving our glory to the true source of unadulterated goodness that is God. Only God is capable of returning glory to us. No other thing, no other person, no other place has that capability. And God is so *willing*! If only we will let him.

Yes, there are many men and women who made great contributions to humanity. They believed in life and they used love to enable them to contribute.

> In all thy ways acknowledge him and he will make straight your path.

Proverbs 3:6

Ask and you will receive, and your joy will be complete.
John 16:24

Chapter Seventeen

Becoming Intimate with God

I once read that you can tell you have reached your comfort level with God when you can see yourself as a child crawling up into his lap and calling him daddy. What a lovely picture. Imagine the mighty arms of our loving Father holding his child; soothing, healing, and comforting him; loving and guiding him; teaching him; and giving him great wisdom.

Some of us were blessed with similar earthly fathers and some of us were not. The loving earthly father holding his child wants to help his child in every way possible; however, this father does have his earthly limitations. Our heavenly Father has no limitations. He has ways we cannot even fathom.

> For my thoughts are not your thoughts, neither are my ways your ways, declares the Lord. As the heavens are higher than the earth, so are my ways higher than your ways and my thoughts than your thoughts.
>
> Isaiah 55:8–9

He loves us, and *all* he asks of us is that we love him. He asks far less of us than we ask of him. He asks so little and is willing to give so much more in return. Why do we, as people, overlook such an offer of love?

Designing God

Perhaps one reason we overlook such an offer of love is that we, with our limited perceptions, have designed our Father only as we are able to understand him. Perhaps because our knowledge does not exceed what is three dimensional, we have difficulty imagining the infinite powers and capabilities of God.

Possibly we cannot accept the love of God simply because it is beyond our comprehension. Haven't all of us at one point or another put God to the test according to our own volition? I personally have told God what I needed as well as when and how I expected him to meet my needs. Then I had the audacity to be angry with him for not arranging things according to my will and my timeframe. I was unable to fathom a solution to my problems that was beyond *my* capabilities; therefore, I erroneously placed those same limitations upon God. How he has managed to be so patient with me is a wonder.

Is it not quite lame of us to deny the existence and love of God because he and his ways far exceed our ability to understand him? The most crucial question that has forever confused us is how God made himself into three at once. I personally have no idea how he could have done it. However, I'll tell you this for sure. When the time comes for me to stand before him, you can be certain that I will choose to say to him, "Lord, I don't know *how* you did it, but I believe you did." I will not say, "It doesn't make any sense to me, so I choose not to believe."

The Price

Perhaps we choose to deny God because we fear that we must give up something that is valuable to us in order to please God. We fear the price will be too great. Therefore, we aren't even willing to window shop in God's store because we are apprehensive of the high cost.

We fail to understand that God does not require us to deny everything except him; he asks that we put him *first*. He does not command that we forfeit our identities and become an indistinct existence. Only when we put him first does his plan for us work. He requires us to look solely to him for our utmost development.

Yes, he does command us to pay a price. We have to give up our greed, our selfish whims, our persecution of our fellow man, and our dependence on the things we cannot take with us when we leave this world. In exchange he gives us all that we need to live, the ability to give freely to others, peace of mind, a valuable purpose in this life, the love of others, and the treasures that will remain with us into eternity. How can we say the cost is too great?

Keeping Secrets from God

I have found that the more of myself I take to God and the more honest I am with him, the more intimate we become. How foolish we are to hold things back from him as though he didn't know everything about us anyway. Perhaps he is looking for us to be completely honest with him and hold nothing back—not even our most vile feelings. Is it not possible that he is waiting for our absolute honesty? For only in being completely honest with him do we demonstrate our trust in his promises. He promises us forgiveness and yet it is difficult for us to imagine that he could truly forgive our pathetic shortcomings. He promises us his peace and yet it is typically human to make things difficult instead of allowing them to be easy. He promises us everlasting life and yet we hoard and snatch our material follies as though there was no tomorrow. We live as though our lives were contingent upon our possessions and accomplishments and our worth is measured by our fellow man.

Absolute intimacy with God needs to be our basic and ultimate resolution. Our desire for this intimacy must be our primary purpose. Without this intimacy were are destined to adversity and hardships.

Intimacy with God does not obliterate all difficulties and tribulations from our lives, but it does afford us the most effective and painless ways of facing the realities of our lives on this earth. When we go to him and express our earnest desire for intimacy, he will make himself known to us. God wants intimacy with us, but he gives us the freedom to choose or deny him.

> He who loves me will be loved by my Father, and I too will love him and show myself to him.
>
> John 14:23

Why Did He Give Us This Choice?

People wonder why Jesus went to the cross when he could easily have overthrown his oppressors and take immediate control of the universe.

At the time that Jesus came to earth, the rulers and authorities had decreed that people would live by their laws or be put to death. There was no gray area; it was one or the other. The laws the rulers enforced were of sole benefit to them. The common people gained nothing by the law except the right to exist. The soldiers of Rome were nothing more than puppets, and the people were reduced to sub-standard existences with no choice but to conform to heavy taxation, rigid laws, and endless rituals. The rulers insisted on having total control, and they killed any threat to that control.

So why did Christ not overthrow the tyrant when it would have been so easy for him? Because if he had, would he not have taken their place as dictator? For to have power over these, he could be nothing short of a dictator. They could not understand Jesus' laws of love, kindness, and forgiveness. The laws of that time gave people no freedom. People had two options: obey or die.

The good news of Christ is that he is not a dictator. Christ knew that there was no glory or value in blind obedience. He, in contrast to his authorities, did not want his people merely going through the motions just to avoid death.

> For sin shall not be your master, because you are not under law, but under grace.
>
> Romans 7:14

Although it is easy to read the Bible and think that Christ is saying, obey my commandments or die. He is really saying:

> Here are my ways. I have come so that you may have *life* and have it to the full. If you want to live abundantly and joyously, learn from me. For if you don't heed my examples and my lessons, you will be as though under the rule of ancient Rome with no freedom to live, express, or create. I invite you to follow me to avoid spiritual death. I, however, offer you more than the avoidance of death. I offer you the freedom to *live life to the fullest.* I am not an oppressor—but I am the *way* to life. I came to earth to give you a clear demonstration of faith, peace, and love, and I displayed good will to all who were genuine.

So Christ went to the cross to show us that there is no value (life, growth, or goodness) in blind obedience. He knows that only heartfelt love and loyalty to him is real. He wants us to come to him because we love him and acknowledge the rightness of his ways. He encouraged people to want to be like him—he never forced anyone.

> …the reality, however, is found in Christ.
>
> Colossians 2:17

Lazy Praying

Staying in tune with the Lord is not always easy or convenient. Our lives can be very busy, and we can become very tired. When we are busy and tired, it is easy to skip the Lord, but this is when we need him the most! From our hearts, through our minds, we communicate with God by means of prayer. Our prayers need to feel effective or we feel out of tune.

I have a tendency to become lazy when saying my prayers, especially when I am tired. Usually the time that I spend talking to God leaves me feeling peaceful and contented. There are times, though, when I'm tired that I will pray the Lord's Prayer or the Serenity Prayer. Because these prayers are so familiar, I have a tendency to just recite them. Often as I am reciting them, there is another part of my mind that is wandering off in another direction. This doesn't feel very effective, so I found another way. I personalize them. Personalizing them helps me to tune in and *feel* my prayer. My two examples are below. The prayers in their original form will be followed by examples of personalized versions.

The Serenity Prayer

God grant me the serenity
to accept the thing I cannot change,
the strength to change the things I can,
and the wisdom to know the difference.

Personalized Version

I am thankful that our loving heavenly Father
grants me his peace to accept things I cannot change.
I know he provides me with the strength to change things
according to his will.
His wisdom is within me in all my ways.
For his love and his blessings
I am truly grateful.

The Lord's Prayer

Our Father who art in heaven
Hallowed be thy name
Thy kingdom come
Thy will be done
On earth as it is in heaven
Give us this day our daily bread
And forgive us our debts as we forgive our debtors
And lead us not into temptation
But deliver us from evil
For thine is the kingdom and the power
and the glory forever.
Amen.

Personalized Version

Our loving heavenly Father
You are the most Holy One.
I seek your kingdom.

I pray you will make yourself known to me.
I pray the peace of your heaven will prevail on earth.
We look to you for our needs,
For you know us better than we know ourselves.
Please forgive our sins.
Help us to practice forgiveness as you do.
Please help us to stand strong in the face of temptation.
Keep us safe from all that is evil.
I pray the power and the glory of your kingdom
May be within us and we may feel your presence always.
All good things come from you.
I thank you and I love you.
Amen.

The words may vary, but I do try to keep the essence of the original prayers. This way I am able to connect with God and keep myself from simply reciting memorized words. I don't always deviate from the original prayer; I only do this to keep myself from being lazy and feeling thoughtless. You may want to try it and see if you aren't better able to tune in.

Pieces of the Master

God created me;
Therefore, I *am a* masterpiece
and strive to live as one.

What keeps us from striving to live as pieces of our Master? Could it be that we have chosen the wrong master?

> Who or whatever masters us is what we become.
>
> 2 Peter 2:19

Our world emphasizes getting. It is hard for us to accept that the things we struggle for and work to get are only temporary, and that if we can't take them with into eternity, they cannot sustain us.

> So we fix our eye not on what is seen, but on what is unseen. For what is seen is temporary, but what is unseen is eternal.
>
> 2 Corinthians 4:18

If we must focus so on getting, should we not at least focus on getting what we really need? Only when we unite our physical with the spiritual to the point that they are always *one*, do we get the rewards and gifts that far exceed the physical—we get heaven on earth. We get God's angels as our bodyguards; we get Jesus as our teacher; we get strength, courage, and wisdom. We get glorious peace of mind. No other master can offer these treasures.

> Don't be deceived, my dear brothers. Every good and perfect gift is from above.
>
> James 1:16

Now that we have examined *me* and hopefully created a desire to have a more intimate relationship with God, let us define the characteristics, benefits, and requirements for the transition from merely *me* to I AM. From here on, let us acknowledge *me* as not united with God and *I AM* as united with God.

We are what our souls and our minds are and nothing more. In this world of stress and madness, of ego and status, where our successes are inaccurately measured by our accumulation of material possessions, and our self-worth and respect are based on our titles or the letters we earn to place after our names, it is difficult to remember that we are so much more than physical beings. Our physical bodies cannot move until our minds order them to do so.

How then can we forget something as elementary as keeping our physical and that which is beyond our physical perfectly in tune? We must take our physical elements and unite them with God's spiritual capacities to achieve a balance. This balance of physical and spiritual is the only thing that is capable of rendering us whole.

This world has been tottering off balance since the beginning of time; foolishly, we fail to see that we tip the scales against ourselves. Yet every time just one person unites with the power of God, he has stepped onto the good side of the scale. Only one by one can we balance this lopsided, hurting world.

> It is the mind that makes one wise or ignorant, bound or emancipated. One is holy because of his mind, one is wicked because of his mind, one is a sinner because of his mind, and it is the mind that makes one virtuous. So he whose mind is always fixed on God requires no other practices, devotion, or spiritual exercises.
>
> Ramakrishna, 1836–1886

Chapter Eighteen

Metaphysical = Beyond the Physical Therefore: Spiritual

Becoming One with Our Higher Power

Some of Jesus' teachings leave little room for misinterpretation. He makes it quite clear that we are to love the Lord God with all of our hearts, our minds, and our souls. He tells us that, likewise, we are to love our neighbors *and* ourselves and that we are to treat others as we would like them to treat us. There are no hidden meanings here. These are his two greatest commandments. Surely he knew that if everyone lived these two, there would be no need for any other commandments.

Often though, Jesus used parables and symbols to illustrate his lessons. He spoke of physical and material things and used them to represent things of the heart, mind, and soul—things that we cannot touch with our hands. Jesus spoke of wealth not only in the forms of money, but in terms of spiritual gifts and guidance from God. He spoke of persecuting enemies that were not necessarily human people, but the enemies within us such as our fears, doubts, false beliefs, illnesses, and animosities.

Perhaps Jesus used symbolism and parables to render his lessons timeless and provide the way for deeper meaning as we come to understand him.

> For whatever is concealed is meant to be disclosed, and whatever is concealed is meant to be brought out into the open. If anyone has ears to hear, let him hear. Consider carefully what you hear, with the measure you use, it will be measured to you—and even more.
>
> Mark 4:22–23

The illustrations Jesus used were common to the lifestyles of the people at that time. Remember that the people of his time were extremely ritualistic and governed by very rigid laws. His stories and comparisons often perplexed his listeners, but the underlying lessons are quite specific. While remaining specific, they are also universal and timeless. His teachings are for every individual. They offer profound and unceasing knowledge, wisdom, and most importantly an unconditional love.

In the metaphysical—or if you prefer, the spiritual sense, the teachings of Jesus offer enough adaptability that we can (and should) incorporate them into every aspect of our lives provided that we interpret them effectively. How do we know if we are interpreting and applying them effectively? One question: Do they work *for the good of all concerned*?

I believe that Jesus used his unique methods of teaching in conjunction with God's vow in Genesis 1:26 when he decreed that man would have dominion over all things of this earth. Therefore we have within the bounds and responsibilities of that dominion the license to interpret and apply his teachings and lessons to achieve the best for all concerned. Jesus encourages us to unite with him and our Father so that we may become all that God would have become. This union takes us from the solitude of *me* to the wholeness of I AM.

Chapter Nineteen

God Is within Me Therefore: I AM

If there are definitive and undisputable laws that govern electricity, chemistry, botany, astronomy, mathematics, or any other science—laws upon which we depend to live—then are we not compelled to believe that there are undisputable laws that govern faith and spirit? In order to secure a solid spiritual foundation, which is the real key to life, we cannot alter the truths that comprise it.

- Thou shall have no other God before me
- Seek ye first the kingdom of heaven
- Love the Lord God with all your heart

- Love your neighbor and yourself
- Know the truth, and the truth shall set you free
- Do unto others as you would have them do unto you

These are very basic, clear, and simple laws with no room for misinterpretation. I believe that God has shown us through the laws of science that there must also be laws that govern the soul in differentiating between *me* and I AM. When we accept and apply these laws to our lives, we are abundantly provided with more than we could ever fathom. Keeping the following verses in mind, let's move on to define *me* and I AM.

> You are permitted to know some truths about the kingdom of God that are hidden to those outside the kingdom. Though they see and hear, they will not understand or turn to their God, or be forgiven for their sins.
>
> Mark 4:11–12

> Then you will know the truth and the truth shall set you free.
>
> John 8:32

Defining Me

In previous chapters, we have examined and picked *me* apart. Hopefully we have discovered what makes up the person that we call *me*. If we have been honest, we have probably discovered some beliefs and values that have kept us stuck, or prevented us from achieving our highest capabilities. When Sue is just drifting or spinning her wheels or hurting or afraid, Sue refers to that limited self as *me*. The phrases used to express my doubts and fears contain the word *me*.

Example:

- Why does this have to happen to me?
- What about me?
- How can you hurt me?
- You have no time for me.
- Why can't good things ever happen to me?
- How can you do this to me?

Fear and worry dictate my thoughts and paralyzed my ability to act. God doesn't seem very near. Therefore to keep a check on myself and to be sure that I am not slipping back into that less confident state, I ask myself, "Am I feeling like *me* or am I feeling empowered by the Lord and attaining that higher state that transcends worry and fear; the state that dwells in faith called I AM?"

We must take good care of our minds, for it is only through our minds that we are able to communicate with God.

The Two Chairs

About ten years ago, I worked with a very wise therapist. She asked me to try to experiment. In her office were two chairs. She asked me to sit in the first chair and briefly explain how I felt in my present situation and state of mind. Then I was to move to the second chair and describe how I felt, believing that I had conquered my fears and that my current troubles were gone.

This took some imagination, but it turned out to be an incredibly revealing experiment. In the first chair, I sat in a slumped position. I picked at my fingernails and had a hard time looking at her eyes. I rambled on and on. I said unkind things about myself. I blamed myself for all the pain I saw and I blamed others for holding me back.

Then I moved to the second chair. I sat quietly for a moment and let myself imagine my life without all these fears and worries. I sat straight up and looked in her eyes. I told her what my talents were and all the positive things I had accomplished and wished to accomplish. I was, on one hand, quiet and reluctant to leave that second chair. But at that time, I was not aware that I did possess the ability to rise above my fears, so I mentally slithered back into the first chair and stayed *stuck.*

She then asked me what kept me sitting in the first chair and what prevented me from moving to the second. At that time I could not give her an answer, and she left it to me to find the answer. Her question stayed with me for a very long time.

Finally, after many more years of struggling, I believe I have come up with the answer. The first chair represented *me* full of fear and worry and, most of all, very *alone*. Although I could not see it at the time, the second chair represented I AM. In the second chair, or in the state of I AM, Sue was not and is *not* alone. She was empowered by a strength that *me* and all of its fears could not even see. The answer in spite of all the troubles that ensued while I was searching for it - had to come from within Sue. I am thankful that my counselor was wise enough not to give me the answer but let me find it for myself, because the impact of discovering this power within myself, I was and continue to be an ever-unfolding source of strength.

Define I Am

I have taken monumental steps in learning who I am when I determined irrefutably that:

> ... and that I myself may be in them.
>
> John 17:21

We exist *only* because God created us in his image and offered to us all that he is through his Holy Spirit. We are what God is. All the goodness, wisdom, strength, and grace of God is available to the person that God created us to be. He put his wonderful gifts within us, and he seeks their expression through us. He gives us the freedom to be with or without him.

God in the human form of Jesus Christ beautifully shows us how to live as I AM. I AM far exceeds the potential of *me*. I AM has no limitations; I AM is free; I AM is sure and confident. I AM is not afraid.

> I shall fear not for thou art always with *me*.
>
> Psalm 23:4

When I lose sight of the fact that God is actually within me, or when I fail to focus on the spiritual part of myself, I relapse into *me*. When I relapse into *me*, the extraordinary gifts of the Lord become inaccessible. These are the time when I can't seem to find the Lord. I scream for him so loudly and I panic so that I can't find him.

He didn't leave; *I allowed my faith to falter*. When I allow my faith to falter, the louder I scream, the further away he seems. I must be quiet, stop screaming, and remember his promise.

> Be still and know that I am God.
>
> Psalms 46:10

When the balance between physical and spiritual is upset, *me* dominates. When I am not united with my ever-present Lord, the inadequacies of *me* take control.

Undeviating awareness of our indwelling God creates I AM, and I AM:

- is unequivocally aware of the oneness with God
- does not give in to fear

> Be still and know that I am God.
>
> Psalm 46:10

- sees beauty

> He has made everything beautiful in its time.
>
> Ecclesiastes 3:11

- does not question what is not yet meant to be known, but trusts

> Don't be afraid, just trust me.
>
> Mark 5:36

- believes that all that I AM needs to know at any given time will be available

> For the Holy Spirit will teach you at that time what you should say.
>
> Luke 12:12

- is peaceful

> Peace I leave you; my peace I give to you.
>
> John 12:27

- is guided in all ways.

> In all your ways acknowledge him, and he will make your path straight.
>
> Proverbs 3:6

- believes that God can do ALL things and that God has ways we know not of .

> ... but with God all things are possible.
>
> Matthew 19:26

- creates
- is empowered
- rejoices in all that is good
- does not acknowledge; therefore gives no power to anything that is unlike God; in other words, anything that is unlike I AM
- is always now, in the present moment
- does not worry or dread through procrastination
- can only be empowered to the same extent to which we are able to make room for God

> According to your faith it shall be done to you.
>
> Matthew 9:29

My constant prayer is: "Let my oneness with God create, develop, and sustain all that I AM according to his purpose."

When we are empowered by God within, we display love. We are not compelled to think, feel, or do or say anything that isn't of love. First Corinthians 13:4–8 tells what love is.

Love is patient and kind;
It is not jealous or conceited or proud.
Love is not ill mannered or selfish or irritable.
Love does not keep a record of wrongs.
Love is not happy with evil, but his happy with truth.
Love never gives up; and it is faith,
Hope and patience never fail.
Love never fails.

Affirm: God is love.

All is available to us when we release *me* and trust God to create and sustain I AM. A conscious decision empowered with heartfelt desire to achieve the state of I AM is required.

We need to ask God to fill us with the desires that are his and learn to recognize that they do come from him. We must make a conscious decision to hear and heed those desires-make a dedicated commitment to release all desires that come from *me* and tune in with God's desires. God's desires for us are good.

> All things work for the good of those who are called to his purpose.
>
> Romans 8:28

When desire comes only from God and we recognize it as such, we can put our absolute faith into God and know that he *will* enable us to achieve those desires. God's desires for us are good and he is glad to give his assistance to their fulfillment.

> So that the man of God may be thoroughly equipped for every good work.
>
> 2 Timothy 3:17

Any desires unlike the qualities of God—those to hurt anyone, even ourselves, cannot be the desires of God. To give in to these ill desires is to do so against what God is, against what we strive to be and these ill desires are destined to come back to us in ill ways.

I AM releases the need to achieve satisfaction that is obtained by taking any thing from anyone else. For to focus on and to map our courses in accordance with things that are godlike is the only way to truly get and then God is happy to help.

> But seek first his kingdom and his righteousness, and all these things will be given to you as well.
>
> Matthew 6:33

Our Storehouses

I AM builds and stores the thing that cannot be taken from us. Throughout our lives we will be confronted by people whose desire it is to take things from us. They may succeed in taking from us our money, our material possessions, our dignity, and our freedoms. But no one can take from us our faith, our knowledge, or our indwelling God,

> If a man empties his purse into his head, no one can take it from him.
>
> Benjamin Franklin

> For where your treasure is, there your heart will be also.
>
> Luke 12:34

Whose Business Is It Anyway?

I AM is content to entrust the business of other's to the Lord. When we become I AM, we no longer fret over others but pray for the Lord to fill our souls and our beings with his love, wisdom, patience, kindness, and the ability to detach ourselves from the entanglement of other's problems. When we confidently accept these peaceful qualities, we enable ourselves to offer genuine concern and assistance. Then it is possible for all to see objective solutions and not be overwhelmed by the problems. We ask God to illuminate us so that we shine in the presence of others—thereby creating a desire within them to emulate what is good from within us so that they too may shine. I AM demonstrates rather than dictates. Demonstrations create desire and dictations create resistance.

The business of others is best handled by God. If we truly want to help others in the most effective way, we need to go over their head straight to God. We can best mind the business of others, as well as our own, by lifting all of our concerns to the Lord. Jesus did not go around sticking his nose into other people's problems. He showed compassion, prayed for their well-being, and demonstrated the way of peace.

> As I have loved you, so you must love on another.
>
> John 13:34

Only Be Willing

> ... and God is able to make grace abound you, so that in all things at all times have all that you need, you will abound in every good work.
>
> 2 Corinthians 9:8

When we ask the Lord to fill our souls and our beings with his qualities, we must only desire and be willing to release all the characteristics of *me*. This must be one reason the Lord said,

> And when you stand praying, if you hold anything against anyone, forgive him, so that your Father in heaven may forgive your sins.
>
> Mark 11:25

We must rid ourselves of our junk. For if we go to the Lord with less than an empty container how can we expect him to fill it? If our containers (our souls) are congested and muddled with anger, the need for revenge, jealousy, envy, fear or anything that is uncharacteristic of God, then we cannot expect the Lord to fill our containers (souls) with the good things we seek, for we have no room for them. We are not giving the Lord enough room. We must first empty ourselves.

> I tell you the truth, unless you change and become like little children, you will never enter the kingdom of heaven. Therefore, whoever humbles himself like this child is the greatest in the kingdom of heaven.
>
> Matthew 18:3–4

We must empty ourselves and clean ourselves out to the point that we are as fresh, new, innocent and trusting in the Lord as little children, otherwise we are too cluttered for the Lord to fill us.

All that is required is the willingness and the honest desire to empty ourselves. If we are filled with junk, all we need to do is to truly desire to be rid of it. We may not know how, but the desire to be rid of our mental rubbish (which is anything unlike God) has to be a desire from God Himself. When it is God's desires that we experience, we can be sure that he *will* help us accomplish them. It is the good desire itself that creates the way for the means.

> With man this is impossible, but not with God; all things are possible with God.
>
> Mark 10:27

We need to take inventory of our inner possessions-like cleaning the closet and deciding what to keep, what to polish, and what to throw away. This may take time and work, but it is work that is guaranteed to be highly profitable.

Some may be open minded enough to simply act upon the desire to release all the junk indiscriminately. They may be able to pack it all up and throw it to the heavens for transformation—transformation from junk to light and peace.

Yet, others of us may have to be more definitive and release identified parcels of junk as we learn to recognize and define them. This is a lifelong process and may require frequent releasing in steps, as it becomes necessary, but always seeking a higher plateau, always working to make more room for the Lord. He cannot fill us unless we empty ourselves of our clutter and make room for him.

Where there is hate, there is no room for God. In spite of the dire need for God, there is no room for God where there is hate, anger, jealousy, blame, fear, greed, false pride, egotism, rage, lust, and all like things. God is none of these things. Jesus instructs us to make peace with our enemies; inner as well as outer. He is not telling us to do this because he is requiring us to be ceremonious or asking us to perform certain rituals in order to worthy of his help, but he is telling us that he cannot fill us with his love if we are cluttered and clogged up with things that obstruct his work within us. How can he help us if we give power that is rightfully his, to our problems instead of him?

Make no mistake. I AM is still tempted, but I AM is strengthened and guided in all ways by the Lord, therefore I AM is able to resist. I AM is not perfect and is still human, but through God's grace, I AM works.

How Much Power Do We Give the Lord?

We will never ask ourselves a more important question, because the extent to which we may become empowered can only be equivalent to the amount of power that we give to the Lord.

According to your faith will it be done to you.
Matthew 9:29

According to your faith. Serious consideration should be given to these four words According to your faith…

Where do we put our faith and how much power do we give it? The more power we give it, the more power it has. As much as we are able to believe is the extent to which we may expect. We need to start all over and put our faith in its rightful place. We must give total faith to nothing and no one but God lest we allow things that are unlike God to have any power over us. We need to start over and trust that it is safe to place our faith with God.

If we want to live life to the fullest, have total peace of mind, know that we are guided in all our ways, know that God truly wants the best for us; if we want to walk with our heads up, if we want to have a song in our hearts, if we want peace of mind, if we want enlightenment and fulfillment of our souls, please consider the following:

God the Master Artist

We must give him formless clay to shape—we must be pliable. For the Lord will take our formless, pliable clay-like beings and mold, fashion, and polish us into works of beauty. We cannot go to him with our own design.

…does the clay say to the potter, what are you making?
Isaiah 34:9

We must let him create the design, then we are assured and we can count on him to fashion us and decorate us like an artist creates a masterpiece. For are we not actually pieces of the Master himself? An artist who takes pride in his work is not satisfied with an incomplete picture. He needs to make it complete. He decorates his works with the finest of materials and puts into it his own heart and soul. His work is a demonstration of his love.

If we truly desire to be one with God—therefore I AM—then let us think of ourselves as his raw material. Let us place our raw materials (our souls and our entire beings) in the hands of the Master Artist so that he can transform each of us into his own unique work of art.

> ... can I not do with you as this potter does? declares the Lord. Like clay in the hand of the potter, so are you in my hand.
>
> Jeremiah 18:6

God the Master Builder

And/or let us think of him as the Master Builder—taking our integrity, our values, our character, and our bodies and transforming them into a home that is beautiful inside and out—a temple for our souls.

God the Master Technician

And/or let us see God as the Master Technician who puts all of our components (our capabilities) together to form an intricate mechanism that serves valuable and viable functions, one that is quite unique.

God the Loving Father

And/or let us see God as the loving Father who takes his newborn infant and raises him in love and teaches him to be wise and kind, and give him so much love, attention, guidance, comfort, and wisdom that the child matures into an adult who is loving, kind, giving, non-judgmental, productive, a mature adult who shines and whose illumination lights his own path as well as the paths for others, a complete person who is filled with such inspiration that he inspires others, a complete person whose oneness with God instills in others the perpetual desire to shine.

The end of *me*
creates
The beginning of I AM

Author's note: The author wishes to make known that she can no longer tolerate Prozac but that it did give her fifteen wonderful years. The ensuing years have been a trial and error process in an attempt to be properly treated for depression and more so for anxiety. After seven years, she has found it again. Here comes another book! Don't give up!

Bibliography

Beattie, Melody. *Codependent No More: How to Stop Controlling Others and Start Caring for Yourself.* San Francisco: Harper & Row Publishers, Inc., 1987.

————. *Beyond Codependency: And Getting Better All the Time.* San Francisco: Harper & Row, Publishers Inc., 1989.

————. *Codependent's Guide to the Twelve Steps: How to Find the Right Program for You and Apply Each of the Twelve Steps to Your Own Issues.* New York: Prentice Hall Press 1990.

Dyer, Wayne W. *You'll See It When You Believe It.* New York: William Morrow and Company 1989.

Ellsworth, Barry A. *Living in Love with Yourself.* Salt Lake City, Utah: Breakthrough Publishing, 1988.

Fox, Emmet. *The Ten Commandments.* New York: Harper & Row Publishers Inc., 1953.

———. *The Sermon on the Mount.* New York: Harper & Row Publishers Inc., 1934.

Holmes, Marjorie. *Two From Galilee.* New York: Bantam Books, 1974.

———. *Three From Galilee.* New York: Bantam Books, 1986.

———. *The Messiah.* New York: Harper & Row Publishers, 1987.

Hay, Louise. *You Can Heal Your Life.* Santa Monica, California: Hay House, Inc., 1984.

Mandino, Og. *The Christ Commission.* New York: Bantam Books, 1980.

———. *The Choice.* New York: Bantam Books, 1980.

Peale, Norman Vincent. *You Can If You Think You Can.* New York: Prentice Hall Press, 1986.

Siegel, Bernie S. *Love, Medicine and Miracles.* New York: Harper & Row, Publishers, 1986.

e|LIVE

---

listen|imagine|view|experience

AUDIO BOOK DOWNLOAD INCLUDED WITH THIS BOOK!

In your hands you hold a complete digital entertainment package. Besides purchasing the paper version of this book, this book includes a free download of the audio version of this book. Simply use the code listed below when visiting our website. Once downloaded to your computer, you can listen to the book through your computer's speakers, burn it to an audio CD or save the file to your portable music device (such as Apple's popular iPod) and listen on the go!

How to get your free audio book digital download:

1. Visit www.tatepublishing.com and click on the e|LIVE logo on the home page.
2. Enter the following coupon code: a759-2da5-d816-b527-bc37-6b1e-8b5b-6ed3
3. Download the audio book from your e|LIVE digital locker and begin enjoying your new digital entertainment package today!